Transform Stress, Anxiety, & Depression

Jennie de Vine

Testimonials

I began seeing Jennie for therapeutic support for complex-PTSD 18 months ago. As a NDIS participant, I have had the opportunity to try several different modalities to support myself with this intense condition. Being with Jennie was the first time I felt more than simply supported enough to just get by; actual healing of my condition was taking place, and I was finally moving from basic surviving to thriving in my life.

I can't recommend Jennie highly enough. She is an incredible balance of grounded knowledge, reliability, and kindness, mixed with the deep wisdom and beautiful energy that she brings to her healing support work. The space that she has created at her healing centre is transformative. Just by being there, I found my levels of hope for the future increase.

The sessions Jennie offers range from simply offering a place to feel nourished and relaxed to delving deeper into the core issues and bringing them to the surface for healing. Even in crisis mental health moments, I sought out Jennie's support, and I was always brought back to a more stable, grounded space by her treatments. This care happens in such a gentle way that I never needed to be retraumatised to address these things.

Initially, I benefitted from weekly treatments for some months, then I moved onto treatments only when something came up for me. I was also served greatly from the group workshops and courses that Jennie runs, which I was supported by NDIS to attend.

Through the work I have done with Jennie, I am now able to find tools in my own toolbox to manage things that come up for me, and I am reaching out less and less to her. So 18 months on, I am seeing significant lasting change in regards to my PTSD from working with her. The spaces between my trauma triggers have lessened considerably. When they do come up, I have a sense of understanding within myself and I know what needs to take place to support my health. I am deeply grateful to have had access to this therapy and support as it has improved the quality of my life considerably.

Victoria McKay

Earlier this year when I was diagnosed with cancer, I was introduced to Jennie. Jennie was the light and wisdom I needed in this time. I was riddled with cancer, but the results I received in a very short time by working with Jennie was nothing short of a miracle. Jennie was and continues to be a great support. I cannot thank Jennie enough for giving my life new meaning and awakening parts of me that I never knew existed. Jennie, you are an angel, and I thank you for everything 💜✨💜

Have a blessed day 💜😇

Alison H

I first consulted Jennie for her Universal Reiki as I was having an extremely difficult time with serious family, health, and my own anxiety and depression issues. I had heard of Reiki, but I wasn't sure what it entailed. As medication and counselling weren't really helping me because I was so emotionally and physically unwell, I decided to give Reiki a try. I found Jennie and went to my first session with an open mind.

Wow–that first healing session was amazing. I came away from it with a completely different outlook on life and with all my anger, anxiety, and stresses gone. I have opened my heart and mind to my spiritual side, and I can't believe what a complete turnaround I have had from doing this. My friends and family can't believe the difference in me; life is now worth waking up for each day.

The situations in my family life haven't really changed, but I can now deal with these issues in a much better way without causing myself worry, anxiety, and stress. I have learnt through Jennie to take one day as it comes and not to worry about what "might" happen in my life.

I have since had one further healing with Jennie, which has just cemented what I have learnt and felt. I will continue to see Jennie for a little while longer.

I can highly recommend Jennie for healing. She is a lovely lady with a very kind, gentle heart and soul, whom I connected with immediately. She has made a huge difference in my life, and for that I thank her each and every day. I can now go forward and live my life to the fullest.

Marlise Vickery

Rise Above Life: Transform Stress, Anxiety & Depression.

(Jennie de Vine) © 2023

https://www.diamondlighthealingcentre.com.au

The moral rights of Jennie de Vine to be identified as the author of this work have been asserted in accordance with the Copyright Act 1968.

First published in Australia 2023 by Diamond Light Healing Centre.

https://www.diamondlighthealingcentre.com.au

ISBN 978-0-6458895-8-1

Any opinions expressed in this work are exclusively those of the author and are not necessarily the views held or endorsed by Diamond Light Healing Centre.

All rights reserved. No part of this publication may be reproduced or transmitted by any means, electronic, photocopying or otherwise, without prior written permission of the author.

Disclaimer

All the information, techniques, skills and concepts contained within this publication are of the nature of general comment only, and are not in any way recommended as individual advice. The intent is to offer a variety of information to provide a wider range of choices now and in the future, recognising that we all have widely diverse circumstances and viewpoints. Should any reader choose to make use of the information herein, this is their decision, and the author and publisher/s do not assume any responsibilities whatsoever under any conditions or circumstances. The author does not take responsibility for the business, financial, personal or other success, results or fulfilment upon the readers' decision to use this information. It is recommended that the reader obtain their own independent advice.

Dedicated to

This book is dedicated to my family, friends, many clients, and people I have met on my journey. It is also dedicated to you, the reader; your energetic resonance has called this book into your vibrational field, and my hope is that you will learn and grow with it.

Its reason for coming into your life will become clear as you read and assimilate the information within.

I trust that you find what you are looking for within this book. It's filled with many nuggets of gold.

Much love and light 💜⭐💜

Jennie de Vine
Diamond Light Healing Centre

Foreword

I have been so lucky to have known Jennie de Vine for nearly two years now. She has been my constant guide and her kindness and wisdom have supported me in some major life moves.

There is so much insight contained in the words of this rare book. It holds all of Jennie's many years of training in various modalities. It is a tribute to her and the years she has dedicated to helping clients heal. And heal we do. With Jennie's guidance, we grow in self-belief and self-confidence, readying us to move towards our potential.

Each chapter of the book is like an illumination of Jennie's intuition and wisdom. The title of each chapter serves as a reminder of what can help you heal, leading you to immerse into that chapter for more insight.

Even knowing Jennie as I do, I was very impressed by this rare book and all the simple wisdom distilled for all to benefit from.

You can also contact Jennie for healing as she now works with me remotely, which is equally effective.

This is a book to be read again and again, and I can't recommend it enough. It will be your bedside reference as well as your workbook.

May your light shine more brightly by this experience of Jennie de Vine.

Mary Walsh

Preface

At the age of 20, I was diagnosed as depressed and given "upper pills." After many weeks of increasing the dosages, and wondering why the issue of why was I depressed was never properly addressed by medical professionals, chance had its play: a discussion with a workmate led me to visiting a homeopath. That visit changed my life. I discovered a new and overwhelming interest into the spiritual aspects of myself.

Years passed, and when I developed chronic fatigue syndrome, the medical system failed me yet again, so I reverted to natural and energetic remedies. This included explorations within myself, continuously spending time by myself where I discovered the power of my mind and how I and the things around me could change me for the better.

When I was 40, I immersed myself into spiritual healing and, Reiki a few years later. From then on, I learnt many energetic modalities, mainly to use upon myself, until I was well again.

In 2015, I started Universal Reiki in Warburton. From there, I opened Diamond Light Healing Centre in 2018, also in Warburton, situated in the gorgeous Yarra Valley, Melbourne.

In 2020 it hit me. There was an inner calling from deep within me that I could not ignore: a book wanted to come out of me. At the time, I wasn't even sure what it was about, though I had some inklings it was to do with my energy healing work. It wasn't until I made time for the book to emerge and flow out of my being that it came, flowing and flowing—I just couldn't stop typing until I felt it was all out.

At the time, I had come to the realisation that I was assisting my clients with more than their own personal healing of their physical, emotional, mental, and spiritual wellbeing. I was giving them techniques, pathways, and inspiration to change their life around, enabling them to do what they wanted in life, not what life was seemingly forcing them to do. I witnessed them become calmer, happier, content, and living the life they wanted.

From my diary in 2022:

This past week I have greatly assisted many people in looking at situations that are happening to them in their life in a different way, a more empowering way, a way that challenges us as humans with our limited understanding and conditioning that we have lived with, put up with, and continue to maintain—until one day we awaken, we realise that we can't change our outcome until we change our perception, our ways, and put into action new thoughts, ideas, and begin to change our reality with the implementation of new ideas.

Preface

It was one and a half years into writing this book, and I had just come out of a few months in my life where everything was discombobulated. My whole world had been turned upside down, inside out, through the wringer, and spat out again. It was during this time when I was feeling very heavy, dark, and most unwell that I knew it had to be for some reason. I had to trust; I had to walk my talk. Through these hard times, after putting into place all of my strategies and techniques mentioned in this book, I realised that this time had been another great reminder that these teachings work! So once again, I took myself back to my computer to finally finish this book that I had been wandering away from every now and then.

Table of Contents

Foreword xi
Preface xiii
Introduction 1

PART I 4

   1. Simplicity 5
   2. Breathe 7
   3. Gratitude 15
   4. Rise Above 19
   5. Grief 23
   6. Presence 27
   7. Love 33
   8. Within 37
   9. Awaken 43
   10. Energy 47
   11. Ho'oponopono 51
   12. Support 57
   13. Surrender 65
   14. Chakras 69
   15. Company 75
   16. Sound 79
   17. Thoughts 83

18. Energies 89
19. Food 93
20. Connected 97
21. Reverence 101
22. Meditation 105
23. Protection 107
24. Sleep 111
25. God 115
26. EFT 119
27. Possibilities 121
28. Daily 123
29. Rise Above List 129
30. Gathering it all together 133

PART II - How to manifest your desires **138**
    It's actually simple 141
    Let us begin 145
    Our vibration 147
    Clarity 149
    Extra things you can do 155
    Evolving 157

Conclusion 159
Acknowledgments 161
About the Author 165
What Jennie Offers 167

Introduction

In this book you will find new ideas, understandings, tools, and techniques to assist you in moving through life's challenges. It will teach you skills to use on a daily basis when you encounter stress, anxiety, depression, or any other imbalances you experience. This book will empower and transcend you to a place of inner peace with ease and grace.

I bring new inspirations in this book, including ways of being present from the heart in each moment, how and why this is important, and how it can benefit you and those around you. I offer you knowledge and understanding of how to bring spiritual aspects into your life so that we can work as one, allowing the divine to work its magic.

Please take to heart:

This book is not a quick read with instructions to implement only once and think things will change, and then, if it doesn't immediately, saying it's a whole load of rubbish. Not at all.

This book's intention is to inspire you to think outside of the box. It's about encouraging you to put into practice new thoughts, ideas, and actions, while changing old beliefs, patterns, and conditionings of the past. By committing to the ideas in this book, you can create life-changing moments that will allow you to question all that you do and the way that you do it. It's a book for your bedside table, the kitchen, and your handbag, so you feel supported at all times until you know the tools by heart.

Chapter 30 covers suggested ways to use this book. One way is to read a chapter a day or a week and focus on that tool for that length of time, really exploring it and seeing how it can work for you. Another option is the suggested 10-week program. After reading the book and putting the exercises into place, you will have a list to refer to for all the stressful encounters in your life. You will have tools to use in the moment on a daily basis.

This book is written for all those I have crossed paths with in my life; those whom I have had the opportunity to teach and assist to put these practices into place in their life. They have requested all the information in a book and so it is. It is also for all those who are realising that they are stuck in life and want to change their ways, as well as those who want to manifest a life they desire.

Everyone's desires are different. To have a life filled with joy, fun, love, and abundance is what I desire.

What do you desire? Whatever it is you, can get there.

You will also find that when you are discovering this place of inner peace, you can begin to dream into your life. How you would like it to be? Once you are here, you will find that life is so exciting, you will never want to go back to how it was; you will be inspired and having so much fun.

Part II of the book explores manifesting; however, I will share with you that, from experience, you do need to be putting into practice aspects of Part I of the book before the magic can really happen.

I send many blessings to you all. Thank you for reading.

I hold deep, deep gratitude inside my heart, Namaste.

PART I

Chapter 1

Simplicity

Life is for experiencing the love, joy, and possibilities in each moment. If you are not doing that, you are either living in the past, thinking or worrying about the future, being affected by what others say, or internally beating yourself up about something that is nothing other than your ego playing tricks on you, then stress, anxiety or depression can kick in.

Life is actually very simple when we know how, but it takes a big commitment to ourselves. However, when you put simple actions into place on a daily basis and actually get the real fruits from it—boy, oh, boy—you'll never go back. This is when you will realise that you are creating your own heaven on earth; a heaven that resonates with your heart, one that holds life just as you desire.

There are some things that I put into place automatically each day that allow me to remain in this place of joy, love, and peace. I continually create my own future, with magic happening all around me. This is what I want to share in this book.

It is through the consistent practice of the simple suggestions in this book that you will find your internal beliefs challenged, your social conditioning questioned, and perceptions about life changed;

your thought processes may even do a U-turn. If you are, or wish to be, united with your internal willpower, you will create such a wonderful transition into a new, simpler way of being—a new life containing all you desire.

> *If we keep repeating the ways we relate to situations, then we keep repeating our story in our life…*
> *… is this what you really want?*

Chapter 2

Breathe

Lets begin. It's time to put one of the most important practices into place.

Please take this moment to focus upon your breath: breathe into your heart, fill your lungs, expand your belly, hold, and slowly let go. With this release, let go of the pains, the anxiety, the stressors, and all that does not serve you. Let go of all that is not for your highest good: visualise it all falling to the floor.

Again, fill the lungs and belly with the life force and energy of the divine, know that it is feeding you, nurturing you, and supporting you in your every moment. It is releasing and surrendering the old emotions, the past. It is releasing all that is not love. As you blow out the air, pull in the abdomen to release the stale air, replacing it with fresh air inside your being.

Once again, breathe in the life force and energy, the light and love of the divine from above, from below: allow it to permeate through your whole being, hold it, and let it go. Feel the sensation of relief, inner peace, and harmony—maybe for a small second, maybe for longer. This is an important practice to do each day.

Once you can feel the change within you, focus on your internal divine light; breathe into your internal divine light inside you, in your heart. Allow it to expand: with each breath, feel your light expanding, feel it expanding out of your physical body and aura, so you shine really bright…does this feel amazing?

Each day you do this, you will begin to feel more alive, more vibrant, and more connected to yourself, to nature, and to others. Your vibration will be rich and enhanced in each moment, and those around you will feel this, and it will happen for them also.

I have always taught that when we focus upon ourselves first, put ourselves into a great place, the vibration will reach out to those around you: your partner, your family, the community, society, and eventually the world. This is my dream, for everyone to be shining their light.

Taking the time to be with our breath allows us to listen to ourselves. My understanding is that we are an instrument that the divine plays through. So when you breathe in the divine and allow it to assimilate in your being and then breathe out the divine, it means that when you observe and listen closely, you will realise that this is a truly magnificent experience to feel—and if everyone else is a divine instrument, then we, together, are a divine orchestra, all in perfect timing, supporting each other in a magnificent way.

When doing this exercise each morning, breathing in the divine then releasing it out, connecting to our divine inner light, feeling and sensing into it, we can then ask ourselves: What are we inspired to do in this present moment? What will bring us the most joy in this present moment? And if we can step forward and do this, if we can do this each day, we will soon discover that this will open us up to one of the most empowering sensations: going with the flow.

Going with the flow can inspire us to take an unknown road that leads us to a place we didn't know we needed. Or it could lead us to reach out for a particular book, open it at a particular page and find just what you needed to read at that moment. Maybe you just meet someone who has or is what you have been looking for, or they offer an answer to a question or prayer that you have put out to the universe. It may also bring you to a surprising place that inspires you and allows you to unite with your higher self, which leads you to take another journey, and it continues.

Nothing is by accident. By listening to your breath and the divine each day, I promise it will take you to places that you never knew were possible. The more I take the time to listen to the divine and really focus on what I'm being guided to do, the more wonderful opportunities, situations, and abundance comes into my life. For this, I am even more grateful.

The breath is also important for our physical body, bringing in the oxygen to each and every cell of our being. But if our breathing is shallow and slight, then our lungs fill up slightly, only letting in a small amount of new oxygen, leading us to feel on-edge and out of control.

It's important to fully embrace this practice each day: breathe in, expand your lungs and count to four, hold, then count to four as you breathe out. Each day, increase the lengths of your breaths until you feel a comfortable flow of air coming in and going out.

If you were in my healing room with me, you would observe that most people don't breathe properly. When they are on my healing table, their stomach or chest hardly rises at all or their breathing is not rhythmic. This is usually an indication to me that they have had some kind of traumatic experience, and they have learnt to hold their breath as a reflex. Then, when they are faced with a situation they feel they can't handle, often relating to a previous troubling occurrence or emotion, the memory of this brings in this automatic response of holding their breath. This is often called our Fight, Flight or Freeze response, which refers to involuntary physiological changes that happen in the body (usually the base chakra area) and in the mind when a person feels threatened. These responses exist to keep people safe, preparing them to fight danger, escape danger, or hope that danger will go away on its own.

This is the opposite of what we actually need to do when we are challenged: we need to breathe. We need the life force and energy to be going through our being. This helps us to move through the emotional aspect of our experience. If we don't breathe, we are not able to make our way through the situation with ease. So let go, and breathe, breathe, and breathe. Allow and observe. Be present.

An excellent way of changing your vibration and clearing the thoughts in your mind with your breath is to stretch up your arms above your head, with your fingers spread wide, while breathing in, then, when you push out the air, bring your arms downward to shoulder level with the fists clenched, and repeat this action quickly. You will find that this will clear the mind and move the stagnation in your body.

One of the most amazing experiences and connections I have had was with a lovely man who was extremely conscious in his breathing. When he was on my healing table, we breathed together and I was able to truly connect to his heart and his soul. We were seeing the same images during his session. This to me is true divine connectedness and oneness.

Another significant breathing experience was when my one of my sons was 18. One school morning, he attempted to take his life. I had two other children in the car, and my husband had left for work—luckily for me there were neighbours around. It was a nightmare happening right in front of my eyes. I had known he wasn't in a great place, but he didn't want help. I totally related when I was his age; I didn't want to be here either. But I also know that sometimes we just have to work our way through it. However, I was not expecting this.

Luckily for me, I had learnt that to breathe through experiences like this was really important. All different emotions were racing through my mind and being. All aspects of myself were on high alert: I breathed and I breathed and I breathed through this experience, and through this I began to observe the emotions that were like waves coming through me.

Each moment was significant at the time—different thoughts, feelings and emotions—I was really trying to be present with for all of them. I used my breath. I used the Ho'oponopono prayer. I focussed on gratitude, observing, and allowing. Once again, this situation brought me inner strength. I was able to be present. People were surprised at how I handled the situation during and after. I truly believe that it was due to breathing and the presence that I held at that time which assisted me to move through the whole event and its after-effects with love and compassion, strength and wisdom.

I knew that this experience was for me just as much as it was for my son. I knew that I was witnessing and partaking in an experience that I was going to be able to assist others in at some stage, and seven years later, here I am doing just that.

Luckily for us, his plans failed. Afterwards, something inside him said, "Well that didn't work. I'll just have to get on with life." He had a few years of emotional torture (as most of us do), then dived into many religions. He found one that suited him and has been really happy ever since. We were the lucky ones; he's such a great young man now and really enjoying life.

The purpose of me sharing this is that I used the tools that are in this book, and they got me through. They got me through that day and those following weeks better than anything I have ever encountered in my life before.

With each breath that I breathe in, the life force of the universe comes through me, feeds me, nurtures me, helps me to shine bright, and reminds me of my connection to the whole.
How special is that?

Chapter 3

Gratitude

When we breathe in the life force and energy of the divine with intention, we become aware of our breath; we become aware of how our body has all these internal systems that operate and work to sustain us totally by themselves. We do not have to tell our lungs what to do, our heart how to beat, our legs how to walk—this is all done automatically for most of us via thoughts and messages to our brain.

I begin each day with deep gratitude for this. I am blessed to have all my human body parts, except four teeth. I give gratitude for this each day. It is with this practice of gratitude that I have come to realise our potential to raise our vibration and for the possibility to change our own lives.

From the moment I feel my body awakening—that first realisation—I am grateful for the breath that allows me to be alive and present in this moment. I extend my gratitude out to inside my body: how lucky am I to have a body that is working as it does, how grateful I am for this. I then begin to extend this gratitude out to my pillow, for nurturing my head all night; my bed, for the support it has given me whilst sleeping; for my blankets, the room, the people and animals in my life; my job, my surroundings, my experiences, anything and everything that materialises until I am bursting with the vibration of gratitude from the inside out. It's such a rejuvenating vibration to experience.

I allow the gratitude to expand with each breath I take. I find something in my close awareness that I can be grateful for until my whole being is ecstatic with gratitude and joy. My face has a huge smile on it; I am exploding with gratitude and joy in my being. When I feel filled with this amazing energy, I place both hands on my heart, and feel the deep inner peace that I have created. It's such an awesome way to start the day.

If you have woken with negative thoughts encompassing you, sadness, or you are going through something that seems heavy and burdensome, you may not think that this will help. But I can assure you, doing this practice will move your vibration into a much more enjoyable place.

The vibration of gratitude has been shown with Dr Emoto's investigations regarding the energy of our words. The word 'gratitude' creates a beautiful mandala pattern in the water molecules from its vibration. This has also been supported by the HeartMath Institute, where they found the vibration of gratitude creates a strong vibration around your heart and out into your aura. It can also vibrate to someone else and help raise their vibration.

With the challenges that you have in your life, I am not saying not to be present with what you are going through by any means. Some things take time, but this is a practice that will assist you, and we will come to these more challenging experiences in the next chapter.

When I really want to change my life around, gratitude becomes key in each and every moment. I begin to look around and see what I can be grateful for.

For example, something as normal as driving into a petrol station: I have gratitude for the car, for having the money for the petrol, for the income source I have to purchase the petrol, for the petrol itself, the petrol attendant, for my car, the fact that I have a car that goes, and so on. It begins to become a wonderful exercise which you may enjoy and harness many things from.

By expressing gratitude for every little thing, every moment, we are given so much more to be grateful for … who wouldn't want that?

Chapter 4

Rise Above

When we go through experiences or challenges, deep, deep dark nights of the soul that there seems no way out of, or deep sadness caused by the loss of someone, the teachings in this book will be a great support for you. The techniques in this book will help to raise your vibration to a higher, more vibrant one than you are currently in. I encourage my clients to create their own Rise Above list for when they are in a state of mind that is pulling them down. (Chapter 29 has a copy of my own Rise Above list for your inspiration.)

The purpose of the Rise Above list is to have something with you at all times to support you when you feel your emotions are heading into a downwards spiral. If you are able to notice when you are heading down, you'll be able to consult this list to help monitor your spiral. However, it's important to recognise that sometimes experiences leading to spirals are either too quick or we don't notice—so many things can happen in a chain reaction, and it can take us into overwhelm very quickly. Either way, the Rise Above list is the key to bringing yourself back up the emotional scale. So when you need to, get it out, and take some action. When we take no action, we stay in the same emotional place, which is probably not where you want to be. The Rise Above list is made by you for you: they are things that you know assist in changing your emotional vibration.

What are the things that you know can assist you? Have you ever written these things down? It's better to compose this list when you are in a good frame of mind. Take a little time to write down some things that can support you on your journey to emotional wellbeing, to a state of coherence and inner peace, joy, and balance, or at least, feeling one step better than where you currently are.

The Rise Above list is extremely important. I have used mine for many years, and still do to this day. This is because we all have interactions with others. We all have emotions and responses to our surroundings and other people and previous experiences, and we all have our ego telling us that we are not good enough in some part of our life.

We also have our inner child who has been hurt in the past feeling pain. Our inner child is a whole topic in itself, and I will go into more detail in Chapter 8. However, the simple version is that we respond to situations due to previous experiences we had as a child or a younger version of ourselves. The emotion we were feeling at the time of the experience, at the younger age, if not addressed and dealt with, may present itself again in a similar way, due to the inner child not receiving what it needed at the time.

The healing here begins with us acknowledging this within ourselves, then connecting with our inner child, and seeing what is needed. This can sometimes be simple and sometimes be complex. If you haven't done it before, it's best to be guided through this with someone. This work is very powerful and can change your life for the better as it releases old patterns and conditionings that still affect us years later. I for one have experienced and guided many people through old situations with their younger self, their inner child, and witnessed the potential of instant healing from this.

We are all energetic beings and everything is energy. All this old emotion stored somewhere in our being is energy, and it can be released, through past, present, and future; it's an incredibly powerful experience.

When you awaken to the fact that we are responsible for every aspect of ourselves and our experiences, you will begin to understand that being able to change our state of mind when we so desire prevents us from staying in those deep, dark places for long durations of time. The choice to emerge is actually ours, and this is what makes life more enjoyable for ourselves.

Experiences can take their toll, and we can be in particular emotional states for some time. It's likely we know that we will come out of these states eventually, but we can shorten this time with the implementation of the tools in this book. With more awareness on a day-to-day basis, we won't need to go as deep, and we are not in those places for as long. Therefore, we move through life with more ease and grace.

Especially now, as I write in 2023, life is changing; the energies are so quick. We have to be fully present, otherwise we'll miss an opportunity. We could stay stuck in emotions for longer if we don't have the tools to get out of them—we may even develop an unhelpful "why me?" or "poor me" attitude.

This chart below shows you how, if you put into practice your Rise Above list at the specified times shown by the arrow, you can change your experiences from being long and painful to short and empowering. You may also find that you can cope better in life because you are not reacting as much, and your emotions are more stable. You will find you are having more fun in life.

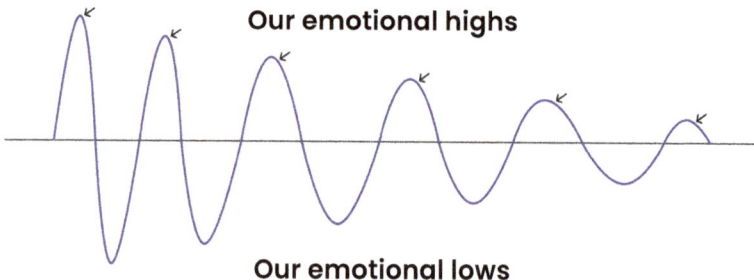

✓ This is where we implement the 'Rise Above' list, as soon as we feel we are beginning to go downwards on our emotional scale.

Life is for living in each moment.
We have the potential to make the choice in each moment.
What will you choose?

Chapter 5

Grief

One aspect that is incredibly challenging is the aspect of grief. Being absolutely honest, I'm not sure that I can fully guide you here, but in this chapter I would like to share with you my own experiences of grief.

The loss of someone close to you is overwhelming. Even though I had all these tools in this book when my mum passed—I breathed as much as I could and put into practice what I teach—the grief took time. And six years in, there is still some grief inside me. Admittedly, it's not as intense, but I feel it. I am conscious of it; I work on it. One day, there may be some more information I can share. But grief has its stages, and the best form of healing is time, combined with unconditional love towards yourself and from those around you.

While experiencing grief with the passing of my mother, I was committed to breathing through the process as much as I could. I feel that this breathing assisted me greatly. As I allowed, I witnessed the stages of grief come as quite separate emotions on different days; each morning another emotion welled up inside me; each day I spent some time being present with the new emotion.

Rise Above Life

Different emotions came like waves in and out of me each day. I was present as much as I could be with these different emotions, and after a week or so, the waves stopped, and I felt more acceptance inside myself.

Each day I was present with what I was feeling; each moment I felt, observed, allowed, and attempted to process using the tools I knew. I kept referring to my Rise Above list, observing, acknowledging, thanking, releasing, utilising the Ho'oponopono prayer (which I'll talk about later in this book), and whatever else I could manage to do, whilst the emotions were present in my being.

Somehow, this process felt empowering at the time, and it enabled me to cope better with what was happening in my being. Sadly, with the passing of someone, there is so much that you have to attend to. I found it took my awareness from what was present in my body. There were so many decisions to make, choices to consider, memories would flood forward. There was a farewell to organise; neighbours, friends, and family dynamics to cope with. I breathed through it all and did my best.

I'm not quite sure what happens in other cultures, but one day I'll take some time to investigate this. In the traditions that I have been brought up in, for the family to hold all of this during the passing of a loved one is a huge ask, emotionally, physically, spiritually, and mentally. I'm sure there are communities around the world that do this process in a way that I would resonate with, I just haven't found this in my life, but I am looking forward to when I do.

I have, however, been fortunate enough to assist some clients through their grief with my healing work. It certainly has helped them immensely. The shifts that were made, taking them to a better place, were immeasurable and profound. I would guide you to have some energy healing work or Reiki if you are grieving.

Grief needs time, unconditional love towards self, to, and from others.

A note on this chapter: when I experienced grief around the closure of my healing centre due to the Victorian Government's choices for humanity, I didn't realise that I had grief inside me since the implementation of restrictions in our area from March 2019. I had lost my dream. My healing centre was now nothing, with no community. I went numb for two years. During late 2022, this grief came into my being. I cried almost every day for a couple of months, but I just allowed it to be, knowing that it would eventually stop. After this release, I realised that the deep grief for the loss of my mum that I had been holding inside my body and aura had also released. I wasn't feeling it inside myself anymore.

Grief supports grief in its release, and it can gather up deeper grief to support you in feeling lighter. Just like when you watch a sad movie, and you keep crying, but you know that your tears are not actually about the movie; they are about deeper things in your life. It gathers up the deeper grief. We are amazing, resilient, self-healing beings if we allow.

Chapter 6

Presence

Presence. This is such an important aspect for us to maintain in our daily life. We spend so much of our time rushing around—do, do, doing so much—that we don't have time or consciously make the time to be fully present.

Firstly, what is presence? Presence is being absolutely still and observing what is actually going on for you right now. That could be in your physical being, in front of you, around you, or beside you. You stop your thoughts and your actions. Your heart is open, and you are totally present for what is happening right NOW. It's an empowering place to be.

When I am present for my pain, emotions, or experiences, I see and sense more than what I would normally see and sense if I just continue to make the dinner, look at my computer, or carry on doing whatever I am doing at the time. I feel that what I see and sense is the truth, and it is underlying what is actually happening right at this moment.

I sense the reason for the pain I have in my body. I am able to tap into the "why" behind my emotions, as well as the emotions of those around me. I find that I am able to see either the truth behind what a person is experiencing, or I can see the "ego" part of a person that is being directed at me or encompassing them. I see that they are operating from a place of reaction, often from a build-up of emotions, which actually has nothing to do with my current interaction with them. However, my interaction has brought them to a place where they have brought in their emotional burdens: I call it being loaded.

The actual issue that you had with them was, in fact, minor, but it has manifested as a catalyst for them to release their feelings onto you—basically, you cop it. But deep down, it's not about you at all: it's about them. These people would usually be extremely stressed underneath, probably not coping, and not realising that they are in that space. They are unwell or their emotional bucket is full, and they don't know how to deal with life at present. And needless to say, they don't practise any of the tools in this book! Just by being present, and in their presence, I can sense this, and I am able to discern what is actually relevant for me; I can address just that, and I am consciously aware not take on the other "loaded" blasting that may be fired towards me.

I must admit a full moon can bring someone to this place if they have a lot going on. This is why I follow the cycles of the moon, as it can affect so many people—and animals. My cat goes crazy, jumping erratically everywhere and running fast all over the house. Vets and hospitals are full around this time.

I am careful with my encounters around a full moon as they are often loaded. In my marriage, after many years, I began to realise we would always have arguments around this time. As the years went by, I learnt to be present, keep clear, and observe during the full moon, as little things could end up being blown up into something quite unnecessary. However, on the flip side, sometimes bringing light to something that has been "under the emotional mat" for some time can offer valuable insights .

To understand what I am saying, you may need to understand what I mean when I refer to the "ego" part of self. There are many parts of us, parts other than the body or the spiritual self, and we also have a part of us called the ego self. This ego self is your subconscious mind; it is there to protect us. It tells us that something is hot when we are close to fire. It tells us when we have experienced something similar before—for example, maybe it alerts us to a similar, previous accident or emotion that we are about to experience again. It can also send the body into a protective or defence mode, bringing back the Fight, Flight, or Freeze reflex.

The ego may also operate from the base chakra or our energetic bodies, which can be expressed through fear, terror, or feeling challenged in our perception of things. The ego can also boost us up, make us strong, and take us into an empowered place of feeling wonderful about ourselves.

In my daily affirmations, I ask "my higher self to guide me and my ego self to support me." I feel this is a very balanced request that suits us as humans.

Another affirmation I use to support me when I am going through emotional experiences and soothing myself, is "All is well." This affirmation confirms to me that what I am experiencing is for my highest good, even though it may not seem so at the time. When you get a deeper understanding of life and its spiritual component, this can be understood. However, when going through emotional or physical trauma, this may seem an unlikely thing to say. But the true essence is whatever we are experiencing in our life has either been planned out by our higher soul to experience or we have attracted it into our life due to our thoughts or actions. These experiences are usually offered to us so that we can rise above it, learn from it, and share these lessons with others in our life.

It can be a difficult concept to grasp. When I was unwell for ten years, I would wonder why I had to go through that period of my life with four children. However, when I reached the other side of it, I had learnt so much about the healing power of my mind during this time. I share these learnings with many people who also benefit from it. So for me, I look back and think, yes, I needed to experience that, even though it was not a pleasant experience at the time.

Presence

Each day I ask my higher self to guide me and my ego self to support me. In doing this I feel safe, grounded, and supported.

Chapter 7

Love

Over the years, I have learnt to focus on love, unconditional love, and gratitude for everything in my life. This can be an extremely hard call when you are going through something tough, but if you are able to always come back to the heart in any situation, you will be greatly rewarded. Love is the ultimate essence of everything—and I mean in everything, including however you see your current experience. Love is the truth of everything; it is everything: emotions, experiences, interactions. Life is a form of love. We are love. It's simple if you allow it to be and complex if you allow it to be. The choice is yours.

If we are able to bring ourselves into a place of love every moment in our lives, then things will begin to change. If we are able to see our situations, connections, achievements, and disappointments as coming from love, then we can take a higher road to understanding life. If, however, we see what we are experiencing as something that we didn't ask for, and we perhaps don't understand why it's happening to us in our life, then we tend to move into a space of experiencing negative emotions and get caught in a downward spiral of emotions.

By bringing unconditional love into each situation we are experiencing brings the light in. It brings in deeper understanding of our current situation. It brings in acceptance of where we are at, then inner peace, love, joy, and fun can follow if you allow.

So, how do we do this?

When we are feeling overwhelmed in a situation, perhaps disappointed with others and many other scenarios in our everyday lives, my guidance is to use your Rise Above list as your first point of call. What have we written on this list is to support us when we are in any state of emotional turmoil. Up until now, we have spoken about the breath, presence, and gratitude. But now I want to take you to before those things…

Before we breathe, we STOP. This is so important. STOP what you are doing right then and there. Then, take a breath, as described in Chapter 2; put your hand on your heart and begin to breathe. It is through this conscious breathing that we begin to change, deeply and slowly, bringing in the life force and energy, the love and light into our being. This encourages a change in state, which is necessary for us to be open to and listen to our heart, to connect to our heart, to awaken to the unconditional loving guidance of our heart for our current circumstances. Holding your hand or hands on your heart brings your awareness into your heart immediately. This is where we need to be; this is the place that will support us.

Having gratitude for what we are currently experiencing is also crucial. Even if we can't see our way out, trust me, this experience will be beneficial to us in some way. Sometimes the understanding is instant; sometimes it takes a little while to drop into our awareness, and sometimes it may take a few years. But, all in all, we will get there. It will be a beneficial experience because it has evolved from our heart and soul for us to experience, learn, and grow from.

It is when we are in this place of unconditional love that we can begin to ask ourselves questions, and we are also able to find the answers. And yes—the answers will come from the heart. It's about listening, being patient, keeping still, and being in a state of presence. When we adopt this state of presence, gratitude, and awareness, then we can allow the information to come forth.

When this happens, there is a greater level of understanding that comes into our awareness: a deep relaxing of our physical, mental, and emotional body. We learn what we need to learn and we can move forward in life with a new perspective.

So what questions do we ask of ourselves when we are in this place? Is this experience my business? Is what's going on the other person's business? Or is this God's (or a god's) business working out in this way? (My perception of God is defined in Chapter 25.)

This is what you need to identify first. If it is your business, then you know straight up that YOU have to deal with it. It's your responsibility.

If it is the other person's business—maybe judgements, dislikes, unaddressed issues—then you can just drop it then and there. Let it go and move on.

If it's God's business, meaning that there is a feeling that there is something deeper than yourself at play here and you can feel it, then you just have to ride it out. All will be well. It will bring you lessons, strengths, and inner peace as it begins to unfold. So once again, there is nothing that you can do right now. Let this go and allow; all is perfect in this moment.

If it's not the other person's business or God's business, then it's for you to look at, and I suggest that you don't hide it under the mat. We ask for the awareness in this situation to come forth. From that awareness, we take the opportunity to put new things in place: either letting go, changing our ways, changing our perception, or whatever else is called for.

"Love is all you need"
John Lennon's song is so true. When you deeply understand yourself and experiences from this place of love, you will understand that
"Love is all you need"

Chapter 8

Within

The next step is to "do the work" on yourself. Own the current situation, take a deep breath, and go within. This can be very scary indeed, but it is well worth the time and space you allow yourself. There are many ways of doing this, but the most powerful way is a journey within yourself. You can do this either by yourself or with someone you trust guiding you. Healing comes from within ourselves not from without.

On the journey within, you will come across your inner child, the most special journey of all. To bring healing to your inner child is so important for us as human beings. Our inner child is our younger self which resides within ourselves. It's a part of us that has experienced all the experiences in this lifetime. Therefore, it retains an energetic memory that holds the emotions that were experienced at the time. (Since we are talking about healing ourselves, I am mostly referring to negative experiences). When healing is done here in this place, it is often instant and transformational on many levels of our being.

How we respond to any situation is due to our knowledge gained through previous experiences.

The cells in our body hold onto the energetic experience of what we witnessed and felt. We usually hold onto this experience if it's negative, and we store it away somewhere within our energetic field—the same energetic field we had as a younger version of ourselves. That emotional feeling from when we were younger, if not properly dealt with or acknowledged at the time, may present itself again in a similar way again due to the inner child not receiving what it needed for healing during that initial experience.

The healing here begins with us acknowledging this within ourselves, then connecting with our inner child and sensing what is needed. This can sometimes be simple and sometimes be complex. If you haven't done it before, it's best for someone to guide you through the process. This work is very powerful, and it can change your life for the better as it releases old patterns and conditionings that affect us. I have witnessed instant benefit from these processes.

I encourage you to get to know your inner child and your inner self by connecting, listening, and bringing in the healing of whatever it needs.

On your journey within, you may also discover some physical pain in your body. Pain is an indicator within our body that something is not quite right— that something is out of balance within ourselves. When we stop and take the time to be present and connect with the pain in our bodies, we can find some wonderful answers, some awakenings, and some divine guidance.

To sit and be present, asking the pain to guide us to what it is trying to show us, having gratitude for the pain, sending love to the pain or saying the Ho'oponopono prayer to the pain, all these methods—if done with love, intent, and faith, it will assist the pain and the deeper understanding that it brings to us.

When we begin to work in this way for our body, mind, and soul, you will begin to see the wonders of the divine. You will also develop a sense of humour as you gradually encounter the deeper levels of understanding of what the pain brings, the signals, and the truths of it all. Sometimes there is action that we need to take; sometimes just sending love can heal many things. All in all, getting to know the pain in your body in this way is a wonderful asset to your own healing.

Any situation that you find yourself in has ultimately come from the subconscious part of yourself. You are experiencing these things for a reason yet to be discovered by you. You will be presented with experiences, relationships, trials, and tribulations to assist you in looking at the way you are responding to life.

This is very important: the more you don't respond, the more you just observe what is happening, the more life will flow for you. I have learnt and am still learning that observation is key; staying in a place of love is key; not reacting is key.

It is when we are able to stay in this place of love that our vibration is strengthened. When we go into reaction, or into a downward emotion (see list below), our energy and life force is depleted. Our ego begins to take over and our experience becomes quite a different one. The key is to stay in a place of love, or when referring to this list, anywhere above boredom.

When we first begin on this path, it is challenging. However, if you remember the diagram in Chapter 4, the experiences will become less frequent, less dense, and life will flow with more ease and grace as we gradually put these practices into place.

Vibration of emotions

This list shows some of the vibrational emotions that we as humans experience, showing the highest to the lowest.

We can move ourselves out of each of these emotions into a higher emotion or lower vibration if we choose. Be aware, sometimes these emotions just move automatically for us, especially the downward ones...

If the emotional aspect of self is affected by a situation, this then becomes a little harder. If someone has passed, or you've had an argument

Within

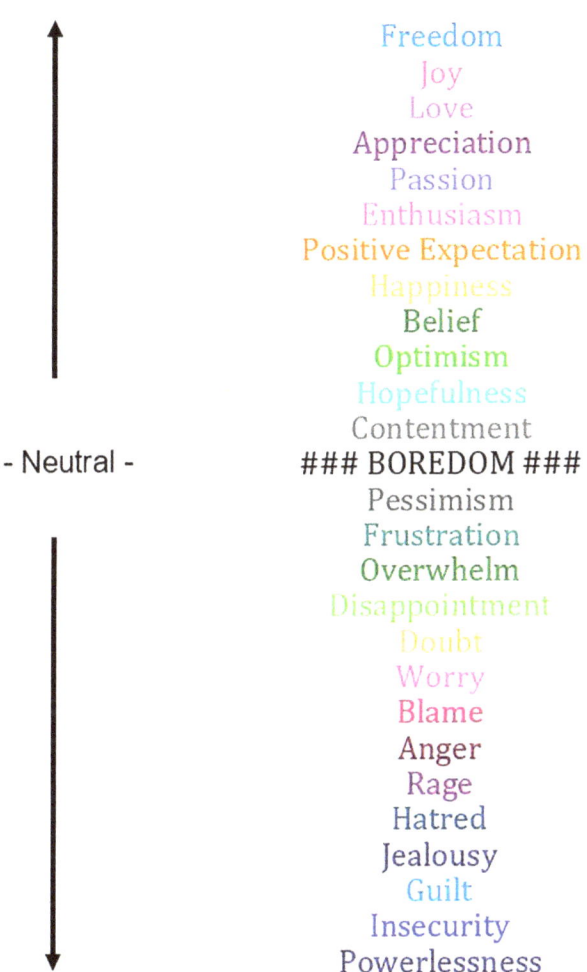

with a family member, it is always more challenging. But always, reach for the heart, always, take a breath, always, search to take the higher road; ask for the awareness and understanding of the situation, and love will prevail. It always does.

Within ourselves are also parts of us that we have put into place to protect our inner child or inner self. Sometimes we have needed a protector, a diverter, or a manager—all of these aspects of ourselves can be communicated with and understood, healed and let go. This is also work which I suggest you do with someone. I have experienced this work with a colleague of mine called Internal Family Systems, and it's very powerful. I touch on it in my work.

What am I experiencing right now?
What is the message for me here?
What does my inner child need?
I'm so pleased I paused into presence and asked…

Chapter 9

Awaken

When you begin to awaken, you begin to understand that nothing actually exists other than pure unconditional love. Stress, anxiety, depression, illnesses, and so much more can be released when we are able to understand the depth and power of love. All these emotions that we experience can be transmuted into pure unconditional love; we let them go, and then are freed. WE have the CHOICE to do this if we so desire.

It is our ego self that holds onto these aspects and keeps us in this emotional or physically unhealthy turmoil. Our true self just wants us to be an unconditional love bunny, experiencing love and joy all the time. What we haven't yet awakened, too, is that we DO have CHOICE. It can happen instantly.

Simply put, depression is living into and holding onto the past experiences, anxiety is worrying about the future, stress is self created from worry, pressures put on oneself and many other things. If we are in the present moment each moment, we do not have depression, anxiety, stressors, if we are breathing into the heart, connecting with the love in our heart, with our divine being these things are not present.

I have witnessed this time and time again on my Monday morning meditation groups: participants come carrying worries, anxieties, stressors, issues, and so on, but they leave filled with love and joy and inner peace. Their whole state has shifted within a very short time. This stays with them until they allow life to begin to creep in again.

If you are in this beautiful peaceful state, then try everything you can to stay there—why not? It's such a lovely place to hang out it; this is my minute-by-minute challenge. If you can only be there for 10 minutes a day, then that will help you. The more you are in a place of love, the more you will become stronger in your inner sanctuary.

In my life and work, I have sat on the fence, seeing things from a different perspective. I have been able to support people with all their different viewpoints, both the ones I have agreed with and those that I haven't. There are, and will always be, things that we feel are right and wrong, just like anyone else. But how does this situation resonate with your heart? That is the key. It may resonate with your heart in a completely different way, and that's one of the things that makes us all unique.

It would be wonderful if we all could come from this place of deep respect and honouring for everyone else and what resonates with each person's heart. What they share may be so different from you, but they are coming from their heart also. Sometimes, however, when one is experiencing stress or overwhelm or possibly trauma, this would suggest that maybe they are currently in Fight, Flight, or Freeze mode and operating from this place. But when one truly knows their own truth, then they adhere to that deep sense. This can be challenging when what they feel in their heart is different from those around them, especially if it encompasses their family or the expectations of society. It's so common, but trusting your heart and doing what you feel is right will always win above all else.

We are pure unconditional love. We are powerful beings. We just haven't acknowledged this in ourselves yet.

Chapter 10

Energy

Everything is energy—that statement from my science teacher in grade 7 hit me the most at school. It was a profound moment. I stood there gobsmacked at this new idea that had my head spinning for days: it was a new awakening in my being. He spoke about the chairs and tables being just molecules buzzing round together, the trees and plants, and, of course, the humans also.

When he spoke about human beings being energy molecules, this is when I just stopped and listened. The rest of the class had left, and I just stood there a bit like a stunned mullet. But I knew that there was something in this. It took a few years to integrate, but from these few words, I began my journey into energy healing, homeopathic medicine, and spiritual bodies. I started on my path of spirituality. It was so much fun; there was so much to explore. I was renewed in the enthusiasm of life. What was it really about? Where had I been before?

I soon realised that my beliefs were changing and they were quite different from what I was brought up with, but I loved it. I was like a dry sponge taking it all in. This is what this book may do for you, or you may already be on the path. It's such an exciting journey to embark on, and it will lead you down many paths of such joy, wonder, and so much fun.

Now, more so than ever, chat around dinner tables is about your energy: where you go, what you do to support your energetic bodies, your chakras, your aura, protection, the food you eat, the exercise you do, where not to go because the energies there are just not right. As humans, we are becoming more sensitive to energies, and the babies born now are exceptionally sensitive.

When I was incredibly unwell, with four children aged 2 to 12, I had none of my family around. My parents and other relatives lived overseas, and little did I know, I had already begun my 10-year journey with chronic fatigue. In the beginning, I couldn't move for four months. I could only lie on my back as anything else exhausted me.

One day, I could feel my mum worrying about me; I could feel her angst at my situation and her need to help me. It began to affect me. I could feel her worry in my aura and in my body. I decided to phone her up, and sure enough, she was worrying about me. I explained what I was feeling and how she could help me. I asked her to stop the worrying and instead send me love. It was only moments later that the vibration from her stopped in my aura and body, and I began to feel a warm sensation around me. It was something I will never forget: the power of love, sending love to yourself and others is incredible and CAN make a difference in your life.

Each one of us is energy—so many molecules bundled together in a human body, vibrating to our own personal vibration that is in alignment with our experiences and our thoughts. Are you aware that our thoughts are energy also? Everything we do, think, say, or mimic is an energetic vibration, and as such, radiates out into the world to attract like magnets—connecting with other magnetic forms that are vibrating at the same rate. This is why some people say like attracts like. If we are not changing our thoughts and our ways, we may experience the same challenges in our life until we awaken and change.

And that, ultimately, is my understanding of why we are here—to experience joy, wonder, love, and have fun.

Everything is energy,
Energy is unconditional love...
... it's as simple as that

Chapter 11

Ho'oponopono

So far I have mentioned the Ho'oponopono prayer several times. I have been working with this prayer for over eight years now, and using it in my weekly meditation and healing prayer group for the past four years. I have done this because I believe so strongly in the power of this prayer to bring significant healing on the varying levels in one's entire being, including the past, present, and future, down the ancestral line, physical, mental, emotional, spiritual aspects of self, and so much more.

Ho'oponopono was said by Morrnah Simeona, a lady in her 80s in Hawaii. She said the prayer to everyone and everything, including animals and material objects because she believed that everything was energy and that the prayer would bring things to a place of neutrality.

Dr Hew Len also studied this practice. At one point during his career, he was asked to assist at a local psychiatric prison with criminally-insane inmates. He didn't see them in person. He just took their files and read them as if he were them, and he said the prayer while doing this. After two years, over 90% of those inmates walked out into mainstream society.

This is a great feat to the power of the Ho'oponopono prayer.

In 2016, I was introduced to this practice of Ho'oponopono for an issue I was dealing within myself. As I began this practice, I realised that it was also bringing healing to other parts of me. I would go for walks saying this prayer in the morning, usually releasing tears as it was a troubling time in my life. Each time I would come home feeling much better. The walking helps too, as it requires movement and, therefore, I'm getting new air into my lungs. During these walks, I would gain a deeper understanding and awareness that some other things, thoughts, emotions, and past experiences had begun to dissolve in my awareness.

The energetic vibration of saying the words of this prayer bring in a balance of neutrality between the energetic vibration of your emotions, thoughts, past experiences, connections with others, and your past, present, and future. It's truly amazing.

I teach this prayer to most of my clients and those around me. It's such a powerful practice. If I'm feeling pain, emotions, discomfort, anything and everything, this prayer can assist me. It's free, easy to remember, and just completely awesome. Do try it and put it somewhere near the top of your Rise Above list.

Here is the prayer for you:

I'm sorry, Please forgive me, I thank you, I love you

You don't have to actually truly feel these words when you are speaking this prayer. Sometimes our emotions are so wild that there is no way we could apologise, ask for forgiveness, offer thanks, or say to a person or yourself that you wholly love them. However, if we just begin to say these words and repeat it until there is a shift in your feelings or your emotions or your awareness, you will find that you will slowly move into this place of unconditional love. It may take one go with the prayer or it may take 20—you may be saying it all day long or for a few weeks. It doesn't matter; it works. Just keep at it.

This prayer for me has now become a daily mantra, though it could be twice a day or a hundred times a day depending on what's going on for me. This prayer is truly so powerful. The more you listen to it and the more you say it, the more it clears past, present, and future emotions, experiences, situations, and pains. I use it for everything. It's my immediate go-to action, and I am so grateful that I found it through a dear friend of mine, Jan-Leigh, who was assisting me at the time. The key is to get the prayer as an automatic response into your subconscious mind, allow it to do the clearing by itself, and use it as an immediate Rise Above tool for anything you are going through. Let the magic happen and your life begin to flow.

There are many people who have created the words of this prayer into beautiful songs and videos on the internet. Have a search and find some; play them in the background as you go about your day.

I really loved it when some of the mums from my Monday morning Ho'oponopono healing meditation group taught the prayer to their children. They would report back to me that their children were teaching it to other children—this couldn't be more special for me to hear. For children to be utilising this prayer and cleaning the pains as they grow instead of being so much older, they have the opportunity to enjoy so many more things with clear energy in their lives, lucky children! Blessed mums, blessed me.

Remember, don't think about the words of the prayer, just say it. It's a vibration. It is key to leave your mind out of trying to understand it and what it does. Embrace it.

My understanding of the Ho'oponopono prayer is that it is a beautiful energetic vibrational exchange which brings emotions into a place of neutrality. You don't have to re-experience any previous experiences or believe the words. By just saying them, the vibrations of the words bring the inner peace. To feel your emotions or current experiences, the prayer can heal the vibration of this. Sometimes I use a song to assist as singing also helps with the healing.

If you're interested in a deeper understanding of the history and origins of the Ho'oponopono prayer, you can search for more information on the internet. However, I have always preferred to stick to the simplicity of it.

*I'm sorry, Please forgive me,
I thank you, I love you.
...So simple, yet so powerful*

Chapter 12

Support

As we go through life's challenges, sometimes we feel like we are going through these alone, that we have been abandoned, and there is no support for us. You may have no human support around you (well, unless you ask for it, then I'm sure some people would come to assist you!). But as you deepen your understanding that human beings are spiritual creatures, you will discover this feeling of loneliness is so far from the truth.

It is my belief that first, we are spiritual beings in a physical body. As such, it is our energetic body that is important to focus on because, as its health and wellbeing improves, so do we. I believe that our spiritual self has lived other lives here on earth. I also believe through a spiritual understanding that we are surrounded by loved ones: those that were once with us, our ancestors, and good friends that have passed. We have guides, guardian angels, and other beautiful light-filled beings that are waiting and willing to support us. These beings are able to assist us when we ask them to.

When I studied energy healing and spiritual healing (and also in my meditations) I have experienced connection with my guides, my guardian angel, people who have passed in my life—the connections are all so beautiful. I have many guides around helping me with my healing that I do. There is so much love for us all from the other side. There is a deep understanding for what we are going through. There is deep, deep love: pure love and support.

I also feel messages from loved ones that have passed and blessings from the divine in so many ways. When my mumma passed, she was at her most powerful. Her children were all around the world and she was able to help us more from the other side than she could in person. To experience the assistance and knowing that it's from the other side is an amazing experience, and I feel extremely blessed.

As I have said before, I start my day with gratitude, then I proceed to acknowledge the support around me. I ask my guides to help me in all the things that I desire to achieve during the day, to guide me, assist me, to help may my day flow, to help make my chores easier, and generally give me a boost. I can only tell you that this does make a difference in my life. It is not until you begin to ask your own guides to support you that you'll experience how your day will flow easier, how problems will be resolved, and so much more if you dare to ask:

- I wonder what wonderful opportunities will come today?
- I wonder what people I will meet?

- What connections will I make that will be for my highest good?

The more I ask, the more amazing my day becomes. Yes, my children think I'm crackers, but each evening I surprise them with the wonderful gifts that have come my way that day, and they enjoy sharing my experiences.

Because I ask with the energy of expectation, that is to say, I am expecting these things to happen, so they do. It's all about like attracting like. I'm raising my vibration and the universe is coming to the party, bringing in what I ask for.

This is one of the reasons that we have to be so careful with our thoughts, words, and actions. Have you noticed that what you think about, you bring about? The energies of 2022 and beyond are magical if you allow them to be.

If the vibration of our thoughts is doom and gloom, then that's what will be in our awareness. If we are expecting that something to happen, then it will happen. From now on in particular, we have to be so careful. People who haven't heard about this before are experiencing this everywhere they go. You can actually have a lot of fun with this. I do advise, though, that you only ask for things you want for you, and for the highest good of others, as universal laws are in place. If you ask for something not-so-good for another, it will rebound back to you. Therefore, I suggest discernment.

In regards to asking for help, don't be afraid. We are actually very similar to animals, and we enjoy being together and supporting each other. I see humanity as a beautiful woven tapestry, with each thread being a new person or a new experience in my life, all woven together to make a gorgeous expanding tapestry.

If you feel you need help, invite your angels to support you. If you feel you need support in some way, reach out. There are always people around that can support us in so many ways, so enjoy the connection. You never know what you may learn, who you may meet, and what you may experience.

When you delve into the deeper perspective of all of this assistance, you will actually begin to understand that all of these beings are actually you, and it is actually you just connecting to you. This might be a hard concept to get your head around, so just read it and let it sit for a while because when you understand this, transformative things begin to happen in your life. You, yourself, are actually the truly unconditionally loving Mother Mary, Jesus, Buddha, and so much more if you tune in and ask.

For most of us, this is not our usual understanding as we haven't been taught the reality of the energetic realm. It's been kept a secret, hidden or forgotten. So many people who used these skills for such a long time were considered witches, evil, or demonic. This information stayed in the hands of a few and was kept very quiet until people slowly began to re-remember and the information began to seep out again at the right time, for humanity to explore and as we awaken.

When you begin your journey of awakening and re-remembering, you will realise that we are multi-dimensional beings and are living many lives all at the one time. This is another tricky concept, but it will become clear to you all in good time.

All of these very old teachings had to be hidden; a veil had been placed over humanity. But now, as the world begins to awaken, the veil is being lifted and people are awakening to it as well. It's such an exciting time for humanity to realise how powerful they actually are through knowing this information, as long as it's used for the highest good.

Of course, there will be people who will abuse it. Unfortunately, that has always been the case; however, if they really knew what was going on, they wouldn't, as it will eventually backfire on them. There are universal laws in place, and they are eternally upheld.

First and foremost, we can connect to our higher self. This aspect of us is us in our true form as a spiritual being of unconditional love in a physical body. It knows everything about us—our whole journey from when we began life as a divine spark.

Our guardian angel's role is to be with us and support us through all of our lifetimes. It knows everything about us and is always a fabulous resource of support for when we need it.

We have many guides in different forms, and they come and go at different stages in our lives. As we reach a deeper level of understanding, our guides change into new ones, who then lead us onto our next challenge, and onto our next level of understanding of our journey through life.

There are many ascended masters whose role is to oversee, assist, and guide. There are many beings of the light from many places including different planets, realms, and dimensions, and most of them are there to guide, support, and assist us. If we keep our vibration positive and our intentions positive, we will attract positive guides and a higher vibration of positive support around us. If we lower our vibration with our thoughts, words, deeds, alcohol, drugs, doing hurtful things to others, then our support will change. Life is always about energy: what we think about, we bring about; what we radiate at—that's what will come our way. That's why it's of extreme importance to watch our thoughts, our words, our deeds, to keep our vibration in a high space because this affects everything in our life.

There are some specific angelic beings who I'll list here whom I call upon regularly:

- Archangel Michael for strength, courage, and protection.
- Mother Mary for unconditional love in my life.

- Goddess Quan Yin to connect with the divine feminine aspect of self, for guidance and for strength.
- Lord Ganesha for clearing the blockages in my way.
- Saint Germain for the Silver Violet Flame that burns bright to burn away negative energies that may be in my energetic field.

The following writing has helped me through life's challenges. The poem Footprints is always in my kitchen to remind me during my darkest days. It may help you also.

Footprints

One night I dreamed a dream.

As I was walking along the beach with my Lord.

Across the dark sky flashed scenes from my life.

For each scene, I noticed two sets of footprints in the sand,

One belonging to me, and one to my Lord.

After the last scene of my life flashed before me,

I looked back at the footprints in the sand.

I noticed that at many times along the path of my life,

especially at the very lowest and saddest times,

there was only one set of footprints.

This really troubled me, so I asked the Lord about it.

"Lord, you said once I decided to follow you,

You'd walk with me all the way.

But I noticed that during the saddest and

most troublesome times of my life,

there was only one set of footprints.

I don't understand why, when I needed

You the most, you would leave me."

He whispered, "My precious child, I love you and will never leave you, never, ever, during your trials and testings.

When you saw only one set of footprints,

It was then that I carried you."

Asking for help is like growing wings and flying, instead of feeling like you are trudging through the mud

Chapter 13

Surrender

The process of "surrender" is also known as "letting go." However, how I see surrendering as totally handing over your whole experience to the universal divine energies to sort out for you. Sometimes in life we get handed really hard challenges (doozies!), and sometimes we do all we can to make them work, and it just doesn't. Often with constant lack of sleep caused by excessive worry about a situation at hand, we are at a loss as to what we can do. It is at this time we acknowledge that we can't personally fix the situation. We have tried to think of all the possible options until we come to a place where we feel our head banging against a brick wall over and over again.

It is important to surrender all the time, with each breath we take, every day in any way. We tend to forget this in our daily life. When we are experiencing situations that affect us too much, it really is a message to surrender.

When we are faced with a difficult challenge, my first port of call is to go through my usual processes, beginning with my Rise Above list to deal with such situations. If nothing is working there, this is where I head next: I surrender. However, if you are keen to surrender first, it's your choice.

Rise Above Life

For me, to surrender is to gather up in my mind every single thing in relation to the situation: the situation itself, my thoughts, emotions, and feelings, along with anyone else's if I've spoken to them, as well as anything at all extra pertaining to this situation. Then I visually gather it into a ball in both my hands, and hand it over to the angels to sort out. I usually choose Goddess Quan Yin, Archangel Michael, or I ask for the Angels of the Light. I do this with a prayer. Once I've handed it over to them, I trust and believe that it will be sorted out. I have complete and utter faith. I let it all go, and I don't think about it again, knowing and completely trusting that it's going to get sorted in its own way. I can't say that this is an easy process, but the more you do it and experience the outcomes, the more you will want to surrender.

If something occurs within your current experience, maybe with another party involved in the situation, I reassess again, and if need be, I send love, do the Ho'oponopono practice to the situation and all involved, and surrender again. It's surprisingly effective. The outcome usually is something completely out of left field, something that I hadn't thought about or could possibly have thought of myself with my own knowledge and wisdom. That's why I love this process so much; we get connected to the universal resources that we are all connected to.

One has to approach this process of surrender from a place of total faith and trust in the universal process. I believe that the universe has my back, totally, and all I need to do is to trust. Oh boy, is this a challenging place to be in! But if you can do this, the outcome can be incredibly rewarding. It's power will most likely blow you away, and you will want to surrender more often.

When these challenging times come upon us, it is important to breathe through them. I breathe in the love and light of the divine, then as I breathe out, I surrender. I keep doing this until the intensity or the vibration of what I have been feeling has come to a place of neutrality within my body.

Another action I sometimes take when surrendering is the yoga child's pose (sitting on the floor on your knees and leaning forward, touching your forehead to the ground, with hands at relaxed at your sides). While in this pose, I visually push all the thoughts and worries out of my mind and heart. I let them go and surrender to the divine process of the universe.

To surrender in the moments of absolute disdain is to hand over to the divine; it's one of the most precious moments you will experience; the weight lifts, faith and trust prevails, and we give space for the universe to work its magic.

Chapter 14

Chakras

Chakras are both simple and complex, and it's totally amazing what most of us don't know about the spiritual aspects of our body and how working with our chakras can bring us so much enlightenment, wisdom, and beauty.

By now you may have realised that I am not the most in-depth writer as I try to avoid complexities if necessary. We get a bit too involved in how things should or shouldn't be, or what's right and what's wrong, how, why, etc. Instead, I want to encourage you to enjoy just sitting back and experiencing life and all the joys it has to present to us when we are willing to experience them. The truth is, I like to make things simple: it's the simplicity of life that I am trying to maintain in all of my teachings and my life.

I cannot bring you all the expertise on chakras that will enhance you on your journey here. This is for you to discover, and it is sure to be an amazing journey.

To keep it simple, chakras are essential to our health and wellbeing as they are energetic systems within our aura that sustain our growth and development because they are connected to every aspect of ourselves: physical, mental, emotional, and spiritual. If we have the capacity to attend to our chakras, whether it be in Reiki, meditation, yoga, or other practices, your life will surely do a U-turn.

There are 72000 nadis and 114 energy centres in our human body. If you are aware of chakras, you may already know 7 of these. If you are a spiritual healer, you possibly work with the 12 main ones. But to know them all, you would be delving deep within the Indian yogic teachings.

Nadis are the pathways of our life energies, and chakras are the purification and distribution centre of the life energies in our body. When the flow of the energies in the nadis and the purification and distribution processed in the chakras are perfect, we realise our divine true self. If there is any blockage or disturbance in the nadis or in the chakras, we become disturbed and drift from our true divine self.

The more we work with our chakras—observing them, learning about them, meditating with them—the more we will naturally change and evolve. I believe the chakras are key to understanding our true selves. I offer a brief description of 7 of the chakras below:

Our base chakra is located at the bottom of the spine, and it relates to our foundations, our beliefs, our conditionings from family, and society. It's red in colour. It is also where our reactions of Fight, Flight, or Freeze come from. Your base chakra affirmation is: I am safe, supported, and abundant.

The sacral chakra, located just below the belly button, relates to our creativity, sexuality, and radiance. It connects to our sexual organs and our divine feminine aspects. It is rich orange in colour. Your sacral chakra affirmation is: I am a creative, sensual, and radiant being.

The solar plexus chakra, located below the rib cage, relates to our personal power, joy, and our passion of being on our path. It is rich yellow in colour. Your solar plexus chakra affirmation is: I am powerful, passionate, and on my path.

The heart chakra is located at the heart. It relates to our ability to give, receive, and be loved. It is emerald green in colour. Your heart chakra affirmation is: I give love; I receive love; I am love.

The thymus chakra is located above the heart chakra. It protects the heart and relates to our ability to be fearless, forgiving, and unconditionally loving. It is sky blue in colour. Your thymus chakra affirmation is: I am fearless, forgiving, and unconditionally loving.

The throat chakra is located at the throat. It relates to our ability to speak our truth with clarity and expression. It is turquoise in colour. Your throat chakra affirmation is: I articulate my truth with clarity, brevity, and expression.

The third eye chakra is located above the eyebrows on the forehead. It relates to our intuition and ability to be aware. It is indigo in colour. Your third eye chakra affirmation is: I have subtle awareness and trust my intuition.

The crown chakra is located on top of the head. It relates to our ability to connect with our true self and be that in our life. It is violet in colour. Your crown chakra affirmation is: I am the developer, character, and player of my own life.

Each and every one of the chakras are connected to layers of our aura, to our organs, and to parts of our physical body. We are all interconnected. It's amazing when we get to a deeper understanding of our chakras.

Yoga is another way to work through your chakras. It can be very powerful in understanding yourself, releasing emotions, and facing challenges that you are going through. There are many forms of yoga, so take some time to research and find one that's right for you. Personally, I do Bikram Yoga (without the heat) as I feel it supports me emotionally, physically, spiritually, and mentally. I adore taking part in restorative yoga with a qualified yoga teacher in a studio; I feel nurtured, held, and supported like nothing else I have ever felt. I also feel shifts through my chakras and experience amazing visualisations in these postures. I'm sure you will find one that rocks your boat.

Chakras

Understanding our chakras is key to understanding ourselves. What will you learn?

Chapter 15

Company

One important piece to mention is about the company you keep.

Do you know that you become very much like the people with whom you associate the most? Have you ever noticed that while you are in contact with others, you tend to take on their words, traits, energy, and personalities?

It is so. In your next encounters, take the time to notice what happens when you are around other people. Do you start to talk like them? Do you begin to act like them? Have you noticed that you adopt similar mannerisms? Most of us do. It's a bit like a contagious secret society that happens automatically.

When you are next with people, just stop and observe. What are these people like? Are they kind? Are they constantly repeating stories that they are stuck in? Are they judgemental or uplifting of others? Are they draining your energy or are they energising you? Perhaps are they invested in the drama around themselves and you find yourself investing in that drama also. It's catchy, that's for sure—there is nothing like a great drama! Listen and observe and then think to yourself:

Am I taking on the traits of these people I hang around with?

Do I want to do this?

If yes, well, carry on. However, if you observe traits and patterns within these people that you now know you no longer want in your life, it's time to make the decision to see these people less. You will be better off for it, and you'll have more time for you and for new people in your life who you truly resonate with.

I remember hanging out with some people for a while, and after a while, I realised that I was swearing and cursing as they had done, which is out of character for me. It was only when I became aware of it and picked myself up on it that I could actually change the pattern that was happening in my life at the time.

At one stage of my life, I moved into a community which had lots of people in it who were poverty conscious, meaning they believed that were was never enough of anything to go around. Before I came into the community, I wasn't like that. But I soon adopted these attitudes and lived with them until I witnessed it one day. I decided that I didn't want to be like that, so I took steps to recreate my life and remove myself from that community. I also witnessed lots of other people coming and going from the community and this was happening to them also.

Once again it is about being aware of your surroundings, your energy, your thoughts, and your words. It's so vital to our wellbeing to be present in each moment to what we are thinking, saying, and doing.

Other choices we have to consider is the inclusion of alcohol and drugs in our lives, which are often linked to the people we associate with. The question to ask is: How do I feel when I ingest these things? Am I feeling like my light is shining? Am I present and connected to my surroundings? How do I feel after the effects have worn off?

Each moment we have is a choice—what will you choose? Who will you choose to connect with? Who do you want to be? What do you want to do? What happens in all aspects of your life?

You have the power to choose. Keep your vibration high and you will fly; keep your vibration low and you will descend. All is well though. The experiences we have are for learning (most of them, anyway!), so we can enjoy a more fun-filled, joyful life if we choose.

Are you becoming the company you keep?
If so, is that how you really wish to be?

Chapter 16

Sound

Om is said to be the first sound in the universe; this sound may have even created the universe. It holds so much power for something that we in the western world know very little about.

Om is an amazing healing sound for your mind and body. It is worth trying this one out. I find that when I say Om, it calms my mind instantly. I include three Om's in my Rise Above list and they really clear my mind and aura: I feel it and I love it! It's such a great practice and one that really changes your state. I recommend you putting it in your Rise Above list too.

The Om sound is extremely cleansing. Om can be said with intention to clear the mind. I find the sound Om, while being said loudly, can cleanse my mind instantly, just like wiping a chalkboard clear with a duster. My practice is to sit cross-legged, and direct the sound to each chakra in turn.

It's a bit hard to explain in words how you say Om, and many yogic teachings say it in different ways, which can be confusing. The best way I have found is to sound the Ahhhhh sound and feel it coming from the base or sacral chakra area. While closing the mouth slowly and gently, the sound begins to sound differently—Ahhhhh then Oooooo when you reach the heart, thyroid, throat areas, then the sound forms a Mmmmm sound once the mouth is nearly closed while still saying the Ahhhhh sound. Oh gosh, I hope that makes sense! It may help you to take a little search on Google or YouTube to get a feel for what it sounds like.

Any sound we hear is a vibration, any movement we make creates a vibration, each little sound in our body is a vibration, and so are our thoughts. These vibrations are sometimes invisible or visible, either way they are real. Just like Dr Emoto's words he writes or speaks to water, each vibration reaches out like a pebble dropping into a pond, it affects us, it affects those around us, and eventually it affects the whole. Just like the story of my mum worrying about me when I was unwell (Chapter 10).

Why am I sharing this? Well, if this is the case, that any sound is a vibration, and it reaches everything, I ask you to please just take a moment to reflect upon:

- How do you speak to yourself?
- How do you speak to your children?
- How do you speak to others?
- What situations cause you to speak in different manners?
- Do you ever use a different voice?
- Do you ever use tones with harsh emotions behind the words?

These sounds and vibrations can be felt, especially by children and sensitive people. I have witnessed, felt, and seen the hurt and the damage that is done to one's emotional aspect. It can prove to be quite traumatic—even one word to a child, and how we actually say that one word, is so important. What is the energy behind that word to the child? Has the word come "loaded" with your own emotions from something else? Maybe something has happened prior to these words you have spoken to your child, teenager, young adult or partner, and it has influenced your choice and manner of speaking?

The words that come out of our mouths are so important, not only to us, but to the wellbeing of others and everything around us. Now, knowing what I have written above, how does this make you feel? It's profound to consider that the vibration of your every word will affect every single person in the world in some way.

It doesn't take very long—half a second maybe—to just stop, pause, breathe, and assess where you are before you speak; breathe into your heart, or if you can, breathe deep into your tummy. Listen and speak your words with love, harmony, respect, kindness.

I know as a mum of four children, life gets challenging. I used to stop myself and count to 10 before I proceeded any further. I knew how important it was to speak with love in my heart. I know that always I tried, but sometimes it wasn't the case. But we move on, and we try and try again. In this case, the most important thing is to hold the intention to change and to do better next time. When we hold any intention, the universe holds us, and we are supported. It becomes achievable.

Animals are also extremely sensitive to sound and the tone of our voice. I have just had a puppy join our family, and I am learning so much about the tone of my voice, even more than when I had my four children.

It's an interesting journey to listen to what we say and how we say what we say. I suggest that you take the time to be present with the words you are speaking, the thoughts that come before the words, and even prior to this, what is going on for you right now. This will affect what you are thinking and what words come out of your mouth. Everything is connected and plays out somehow. Being present in each moment truly helps with your vibration and what you vibrate out to the world.

Another powerful practice is to just hum—yes hum—like the way a cat purrs. Your own hum is actually healing to every cell in your body, so hum away as much as you like: you are bringing healing into yourself.

Om
Let the sound of the universe resonate through your mind, body, and soul.

Chapter 17

Thoughts

Even before the words come out of our mouth, have you ever been present as to witness the process; where are they coming from? What is forming them?

Our thoughts bring forth our words. When we are present, we are choosing our words, but when we are not fully present, we can just ramble on about anything. Consciously observing our thoughts and our words can really change our life and the situations we find ourselves in.

Our thoughts hold great power and they are also a form of energy. Our thoughts are forces, and when put together with intention, we can create our reality.

If you have heard any inspirational speakers talk these days, they all mention about the power of our thoughts and our words and our emotions. It's a powerful combination, even more so now, as we as a human race are able to create our reality in our mind, and when it happens—I tell you—it's so much fun!

Do you know that man's mind works in an entirely different way from a woman's? Once we appreciate this, we can understand a lot more about life. I certainly had many pennies drop when I heard this. There's a very funny video clip you can watch: A Tale of Two Brains - Men's Brain Women's Brain - Mark Gungor

Not only has our mind been conditioned by society, it has been conditioned by our parents, families, our schooling, beliefs, our ancestors, our experiences. and so on. This does not mean to say that our mind can't be changed. When we become aware, we can enable our mind to change and to create new neural pathways, therefore creating different experiences in our life. This is the fun part of my work that I do. It helps so many people. I regularly do this as I have changed so much through the knowledge and understanding of this aspect that I wish to support others along the way.

Our thoughts are powerful, and the more we become aware of them and observe the outcomes in our life, the more we begin to say to ourselves, "Hey, let's change those thoughts. Let's catch them in the process and turn them around."

One also needs to be careful with our choice of words when we speak. It's important that we change our statements into positive ones in the present tense. We need to learn how to avoid saying "no" this or "no" that. It's better to use words that the subconscious mind can relate to and can create.

My rule is keep it simple, otherwise it gets confusing—not only for us but for our mind. In the beginning, the works of Esther and Jerry Hicks are fabulous on this topic. Just ask your higher self to guide you, and you will find your way. Keep observing and changing. You will find yourself picking up other people's words and statements and they yours. I find this is a really lovely act to take part in for you and your friends to help everyone along in life.

This is a huge topic and certainly needs more time than my book can offer; however, I'm always happy to chat and have a session with people who wish to change habits for the better.

I see the challenge for us as humans is to stay focused in our heart and to listen to our body: to do what we hear from our heart, those things that make our heart sing, nothing else.

It does not matter what others think, say, or do, but it does matter if we are not true to ourselves or if we go off our path due to life around us.

Everything, absolutely everything around us that happens in our life that is in our field, that is in our awareness is only there to distract us from being our true selves. I call it "the noise." It stops us from operating from our heart and experiencing the love, joy, and bliss that we can experience as human beings. Drop the noise, go into the stillness inside your heart, listen and do just that, and you will be incredibly happy. Things will just happen for you.

The people you need to meet will come into your life, your soul will sing, and your vibration will be high and vibrant.

To clarify, the noise can be TV, social media, radio, the news, other people, other people's dramas, situations, thoughts, emotions, alcohol, drugs—anything and everything that is around us that is not actually us. Dramas in family life and in friendships are a big part of the noise.

I would like to add something about 'intention' here. If you can do anything and everything with intention, it will really change your life around. Having intention about each moment, each hour, each day, month, or what you'd like to experience long-term creates a vibration out into the universe which will come back to you if your intention is clear and resonates with your heart. Intentions are powerful, but they are more powerful when put into place when the moon is supportive, during a new moon or a full moon phase. Intentions are also more powerful when working with others and held for a length of eight minutes, if possible, then multiples thereof. I learnt this from the works of Lynne McTaggart.

I wish to share this quote by Lao Tzu because it has helped me the most in my life. It is one I have in my mind, on my wall, on my computer, in my teachings, in my life. It's so powerful.

Thoughts

"Watch your thoughts, they become your words; watch your words, they become your actions; watch your actions, they become your habits; watch your habits, they become your character; watch your character, it becomes your destiny." Lao Tzu

Chapter 18

Energies

What are you energetically absorbing and how is it affecting you? If everything is energy, then everything around you is energy: the sounds of the birds that bring joy into the soul, the sounds of the mowers or chainsaws next door that might hum away and grind at your senses, the sounds of music which may elate or deflate you.

Not only these sounds, the supermarket can be a sensory overload for many people: the music playing, cash registers, people in the aisle, check-out workers, the mall, the cars in the car park, the trucks going by, the news on the radio, the broadcasting on the television, social media, or your mobile phone. Everything, absolutely everything is being taken in and absorbed by you. Most of the time, you are totally unaware of this sensory overload—unless you are really sensitive, then you go out of your way to avoid all of these situations!

I have been sensitive my whole life. I chose to turn off the television and radio at the age of 20: they did not serve me. I saw what I thought were such atrocities. They creeped into my vibration; they made me unwell. So I stopped watching and listening because the news just broke my heart each day.

All these noises become a part of you. It affects many people without their knowing. It can accelerate your temperament from one of calm to anger, or it just slowly bubbles away in the background, without you even realising your temper is changing. This sensation can be amplified with the television, social media, movies, or aggressive music. These modalities with their strong sounds, images, or subliminal messages get into your being and they affect you. The energy of the message or program rattles around in your subconscious mind, and guess what—whatever is going on there becomes a magnet for like-minded energies.

Have you noticed after you've watched a movie or TV show and you go to bed that what you have seen plays out in your mind again and again, and you are wanting to know what happens next, or trying to resolve something in your head? Perhaps you become frightened. There are so many horrible movies and scenes that people just accept without their mind realising it. They are numb to it. It gets in; it all seeps into your subconscious mind and into your thoughts. Your mind unconsciously processes these sensations and it becomes a part of you without you even realising. All of these things are energies that distract you from being the real you.

So I think it's time to take a breath, become aware, become present, and ask, "What is in my world? What am I ingesting unknowingly?" Do you want to keep those things in your awareness in your subconscious mind to attract like-minded vibrations? Or do you wish to be present in the moment and choose not to take in particular vibrations? In fact, it's a really easy choice, but it's also a very hard one for those beginning this journey of awakening to the understanding of what has subtly affected them for many years.

Take yourself out into nature: listen to the birds, the crickets, the wind blowing in the trees, the children playing, the river, or the waterfall. Enjoy the beauty of the plants around you, the flowers, the trees. Stop, breathe, take a moment: look closer, look at the lines on the leaves, the shapes, colours, geometric shapes within each living thing. Watch the sunrise or sunset, go to the beach and feel the sand in your toes, put your hands in the soil, get yourself into the senses of nature, turn off your phone, the computer, your music. Connect with like-minded people, and make new friends in a conscious way.

BE still. Take nothing in. Observe.

Take the time to reset yourself. Perhaps have a day without technology. I promise you won't know yourself at the end of the day. I'd love to hear back from those of you who do this. Do you have the willpower to change your ways for the better?

What are you vibrationally ingesting through your eyes, through your ears, through your senses? What do you choose to ingest?

Chapter 19

Food

Following on from the previous chapter, what are you ingesting through the food that you eat? What toxins? What additives? What vibration are you ingesting? How was this food made? Was it made in a huge factory with all sorts of things added into a tumbler, mashed around and squirted out through a tube at the other end, then packaged in plastic? Labelled as food? I have seen some food that is labelled "organic" and/or "vegan." It looks like plastic mishmash. Quick and easy might be OK once in a while, but if you buy packaged food regularly, I'm sure your body would thrive experiencing an alternative, fresher way. In doing so, your body will begin to vibrate in a different way. You will feel lighter, clearer, and have more energy.

Have you ever been to an Italian or French home, where they pick the vegetables from the garden, make the stock from scratch, prepare the food with love, laughter, and many people around the kitchen table? This food is vibrationally delicious, but not only that, all the goodness and qualities of the food are enhanced by the vibration of love that is put into the food. Sadly, these days, we make the quickest meal possible for our hungry family that fits into our busy working lives.

I was blessed to be an at-home mum and I was able to put lots of love into my food for my family of six. I couldn't do it all the time, but as much as I could, I prepared food for my children that has helped them stay healthy and vibrant all their lives.

This food not only tastes different, but it feels different. There is a nurturing sense about it that feeds your soul. This is the food you want to ingest in your body. Food that has a vibration of love, enjoyment, fun, and, usually, cooperation.

When we look at the bigger picture, all food sources are here for us to choose from. We have so much variety, goodness, and a plethora of tastes to entice the senses created by Mother Earth, and once again, we can choose: we have choice. What are you choosing?

Many of our current food choices and habits have been created from our upbringing, society, or advertisements. But when we really look in depth at our food, we might be surprised at how unnatural our choices have become.

If you decide to make an attempt at changing your diet in any way, I would begin with eliminating sugar and white flour from your diet. Try it for three weeks and see how clear your mind feels and how your body feels. I'm sure you will find that you are a lot less sluggish and more alert.

Food is meant to be enjoyed. It is meant to be picked from the garden, harvested from our trees, and created into a delicious meal that is full of seasonal goodies. It brings in the love, nutrition, vibrant energies, and healthy sustenance from Mother Earth, the sun, the moon, the waters, and so much more.

If we aim to have a beautiful rainbow of colours through our day on our plate, we are supporting our body, our chakras, and our life force. Take a look at your diet, what colours might you be missing?

Once I have my food in front of me, I offer deep gratitude for Mother Earth assisting the growth of the food, for the sun, the moon, the water, and the elements that have supported that food to grow. Remember they are all working as one to create that little carrot you have on your plate. It didn't just appear out of a box; parts of the divine and the universe have put their love and care into creating just that one pea. If we get deeper into this, that one orange you are eating has been grown specifically for you to eat, so it would have everything you need for you. Think about this: the fresh crispness, vibrance, and vitality from a home-grown vegetable or fruit in season, compared to a packet of food made in a huge factory, which has no real food in it anyway...food for thought.

What are you ingesting through your mouth?
How does it feel your body and soul?

Chapter 20

Connected

There is more to consider in regards to ingesting our food into our body. There are a few other practices that really make food feel and taste even yummier than it is.

I'm sure you're wondering what that could be? How could you possibly make food any yummier and more beneficial for every cell in your body than from home-grown, made from scratch food prepared with absolute love and enjoyment?

There are several things I put into practice. Firstly, I offer my food up to God, the divine, Mother Earth, whomever you might resonate with. Then I express my deep gratitude, sometimes in my mind, sometimes I do it with my hands in prayer, sometimes I have gratitude and offer my food to the morning sun, which is my favourite time. I also give my food Reiki, and ask for my food to be blessed. All of these things are important to me when I am preparing my food.

I do this because I believe all things are from spirit; all things are love; all things are energy; everything is connected. Our vibration as to how we receive this energetic food and how it's going to feed our human body is so important, and it affects how it is processed in our body. Gratitude for our food can even begin to cleanse the food. Just like Dr Emoto's water, our food can change too.

Dr Emoto is known all over the world for his findings of the vibration of words and sounds spoken to plants but especially water. Dr Emoto has done numerous experiments in regards to how the vibration of many words like "love," "fear," or "peace" affect the molecules of water. Once, after offering the words, Dr Emoto froze the water and looked at it under a microscope. To his surprise, he found that the more loving the words were, the more beautiful the crystalline structure of the water was. When I discovered this many years ago, I was profoundly moved by this information, and it changed my whole perception of life. As human beings, we are over 70% water. If a word like "love" changed our molecular structure, how could other words affect each and every cell in our body? Therefore the whole of us, as we raise our vibration through our words, it reaches out into us and into those around us.

Secondly, it might be necessary for you to experiment on this one, for I can only share my remarkable experience. One day, I was completely present, consciously eating my meal, which was avocado and home-grown tomato on organic millet bread. I was consciously eating my breakfast and I felt super aware this day; my intuition was high and as I was eating with my eyes closed, I was taken on a journey, from the tomato in my mouth, to the tomato plant, and into the tomato when it was on the plant, then in turn to the avocado: it was an incredible experience. I became one with the tomato and with the avocado—such deep connection, reverence, gratitude, and amazement engulfed my being. I'll never forget this experience.

My wish for you is that one day you can experience this amazing journey and share it with me. I'd love to hear which vegetable you became one with.

Our intention is so vital to what we do and how we do it. It really affects what and how we experience things in life. My eating process in this way awakens something else within me, a vibration of gratitude, and a deep sense of presence. These things change your experience of whatever you are doing next. I suggest that you try it.

We are all connected, everything is connected; if you take time to be present, to feel, and explore, you will also find the treasures of the universe are within you.

Chapter 21

Reverence

At different times of our lives, we become aware of the different aspects of life. For me, reverence became a strong experience when I was on the other side of menopause. Like a fire burning inside my body that was not to be ignored, the reverence was strong. I was called to experience it and to be reverent in each moment. Something, which I can only describe as an energetic force, was making me stop; something was making me be present. And within that, the strong feeling of holding reverence for whatever was in front of me, or that particular moment, was strong. I could not deny it, so I just let it take me.

Within this experience of reverence, I was slowed down even more in life. This meant I could witness; I could be; I could hold more gratitude; I could hold more reverence for everything I did, said, and experienced. During this most rewarding experience I thoroughly enjoyed a deep honour and stillness while reverence pulsated up through my body from the depths of my soul.

I cannot express more highly and with what deep honour the preciousness of holding reverence is in each moment. Each moment is so very special, and you are living it right now. If you are present, truly present, you are internally rich, fulfilled, and incredibly blessed.

Reverence means a deep respect for someone or something. To feel this deeply, begin by stopping what you are doing, and be present. Begin by being in awe of what is around you, of what you are experiencing. Begin with deep gratitude for this moment, for the past moment, and for the next moment. When you allow yourself the time, the space, and the gratitude, allow yourself to experience deep reverence; it comes from deep within your sacral chakra, like an energy moving through your body. It's something that can't be ignored, like a wave of emotion coming through your divine vessel.

Many a time I have found myself just bowing my head as I experience more and more reverence in my life. As I hold more reverence, I experience incredible sensations, which I encourage everyone to explore.

Life is going too fast; special moments are missed; seconds pass us by without us even knowing. Opportunities are missed; the pressures to do this, that, and the other are so intense. But what you'll find is you don't have to do anything. You will find that when you step back, when you breathe, when you have gratitude, when you slow down, that's when the magic happens: that's when your vibration begins to change, and that's when your life begins to change into something wonderful—in fact, more than wonderful. One begins to finally smell the roses. Take time to watch the leaves fall off the trees, to see the sun rise and set, to observe the stars, to observe nature and just be. You will be surprised that through taking this time, you actually achieve more. Your life will become richer and richer each day, and you will have so much more to be grateful for.

With everything you do, hold deep reverence in each moment, each second; be present. Your life will become richer in ways that you have never known.

Chapter 22

Meditation

Meditation is key to our wellbeing—I can't express this enough. Even if you partake for five minutes once or twice a day, it builds up what I call your spiritual meditation muscle, which calms the mind and body.

Over time, the mind and body begin to realise that when they can be calm, new neural pathways are made. The more we meditate, the more we have a sense of inner calmness and peace, leading to the body's desire to find itself in this space. We can also create and manifest the ability to be calm in stressful situations.

We as humans are blessed with many forms of meditation. I believe this variety exists so we can choose the type of meditation that resonates with us as individuals. As humans, we are so lucky to have so much choice. I recommend that you take the time to investigate the different pathways of mediation with different teachers, online options, or apps for your phone to see what resonates for you.

I personally like focusing on my breath: observing the life force coming and going from my body. I love to hold deep gratitude for this experience each day. I also like to focus on my heart or my individual chakras. I enjoy presence meditation where you focus on one part of your body at a time. I find this deeply relaxing and calming. It really brings you into presence and helps heal the body.

Meditation can also be focusing on one thing at a time whilst you are doing everyday mundane jobs, such as the dishes. Doing the dishes can be a meditation if you are solely focused on doing the dishes and nothing else. This is bringing presence into the meditation—keep the thoughts on doing the dishes. If the mind wanders, gently bring it back. You can also do this whilst doing other mundane jobs around the home or going for a walk. A walking mediation can also be effective; whilst you are being present with each step, you are noticing everything that is happening in connection with taking that step.

Whatever type of meditation you partake in, if you do it rhythmically, daily, and during the week, you will begin to find great benefits with the practice in a very short time.

Taking the time to meditate is so valuable to your wellbeing. After a few weeks of meditating, you're likely to have a calmer mind, a stronger sense of inner peace, and a better ability to function from the heart on a daily basis. It's also likely that you'll react less drastically to situations, increase your body awareness, heal organs, and so much more.

Meditation is key to our wellbeing. Five minutes, twice a day is a great start.

Chapter 23

Protection

There are times in our life that we can be affected by other people, situations, or places around us. The most sensitive people tend to stay at home, away from outside influences and they often keep to themselves—sometimes they don't even know that this is what they are doing. It is natural for them to be aware of their feelings and they may become overwhelmed when they are with others or at places that are loud and intrusive upon their energies. Supermarkets, cinemas, concerts, and such similar places can really set sensitive beings offtrack. You will find that sensitive beings usually like to be in nature because they find it extremely healing.

I am sensitive, and I put into place techniques that assist me when I need to venture to places that have high or loud energies that drain or affect me in any way.

I work with it by calling in the white light of the divine to come into my body and my aura, and I ask it to assist me to be cleansed, strong, and protected. White light is the space within the universe that houses positive energies. White light can be called upon by anyone (healers, empaths, the devout, and you too!) for assistance, healing, and protection from negative energies or strange vibrations. Do try this—most people can feel it.

Sometimes when we are in conversation with people, the conversation may set off emotions for you, and unwanted feelings may rise up. In these situations, the strategy I use is to send love or say the Ho'oponopono prayer in my mind to myself first, then to the person who I am speaking to, whether they be in front of me or on the other end of the phone to me. In those cases, I send it down the phone line or through the ether now! You see, it's actually our own response to their words or actions that we have power over. How their words and energies affect our being is what we need to deal with. How you react or what you feel is your responsibility, and remember, your reaction or feeling may be related to past experiences. This is all OK. We stop, we breathe, place a hand on our heart, identify, then work through our list to shift the emotions. If we need to do it again, we just do it again, and so on.

If I've been somewhere and I'm feeling yucky or negative due to the conversations happening, then I can choose the white light to help me with my emotions. I can also ask the divine for the Silver Violet Flame to come under me like a fire and burn away all the negative energies that are within my physical and spiritual being. Do this until you feel different. Sometimes I take a shower or jump in the river and totally immerse myself as this cleanses our aura and revitalises us, helping us begin again refreshed and renewed.

Other times, I sink into a bath with Himalayan Pink Salt and rub it all over my body and through my hair: this is a wonderful cleanser.

Sometimes we meet people who affect us too much for our liking—we can literally 'feel' them taking our energy away or sucking us dry. When this is happening, we can put in the above techniques. But if nothing changes, we also may need to undergo a spiritual disconnection process with an energy healer of some kind. Remember, all is well. We are learning and are on the path to awakening. Just asking for help is empowering in itself.

Energetic protection is an option for those who are affected by energies around them or places that they go.

Chapter 24

Sleep

Sleep is such a precious thing for our wellbeing, our body, our mind, and our soul. So many of us spend many hours not sleeping and delaying sleep, diverting ourselves with mindless screens, movies, scrolling on Facebook or Instagram—anything to avoid engaging with ourselves in a healthy way.

Do you know that the most important hours of sleep for your body are between 10pm and 2am? I know it may be a struggle, but even if you change this in your life, you will feel different. The hours between 10pm and 2am is where we get the most beneficial hormonal secretions and recovery for our bodily systems. Our stress glands (adrenals) rest and recharge the most between 11pm and 1am, while melatonin production is highest from 10pm to 2am. It is really important to aim to regulate your circadian rhythms (your sleep/wake cycle) by going to bed at the same time each night.

It is also important to not have the back light of your devices shining into your eyes, so turn off your devices at 9pm or earlier the better, make your way gradually into sleep. To have a candle going with it's nice gentle red light is a lovely way to go into sleep (blow it out of course). The blue light that is emitted from your technological devices affects your melatonin production, which controls your circadian rhythms, (your sleep wake cycle) the light can make it more difficult for you to sleep, and can make it even more difficult to concentrate and keep awake the next day.

I come from a family of bad sleepers, and sometimes I find it hard to get to sleep. Firstly, when I am aware that I am not sleeping, I check where the moon is in its cycle. If the moon is coming up to a full moon or a new moon, I have noticed that I can be kept awake by these energies. I believe this happens to help us witness the emotional state we are currently in and process and move through emotions.

Doing some gentle exercise before bed also helps. Some yoga poses can help you relax. Child's pose is effective as it gets the blood to your head and helps to clear it out. With this pose, I sometimes visualise all my unnecessary thoughts leaving through my head until they are all gone.

You can rock yourself to sleep: hold yourself in your arms in a loving pose, and rock gently and rhythmically.

If the mind is busy, we can move the feet. This brings the awareness and energy down out of our head and into the feet, helping stop the chattering in our mind.

Try to meditate before sleep. You can try by yourself or have a look at the many meditations available now on various apps to support you (but try to avoid the blue light).

There is also the option of sound wave music which helps to enhance your mind waves to slow down and go into the delta state where sleep happens.

I also like to focus on my breath; the life force that enables me to be here. It brings the mind into focus on one thing instead of letting it run wild. Maybe even focus the eyes to the third eye in between the eyebrows; just be, surrender, and allow your body to go through its process.

You can focus your attention on one thought: peace, love, kindness. See if that will take you into your dream state.

I have also been practising saying to myself, "Be Still" over and over again. I find that my mind listens to me, and it stills itself.

Self-massage is a lovely thing to do, or if you have a partner, ask for some loving massage.

A warm bath helps to release the tensions and calm the mind and body before sleep.

There is a product called Rescue Remedy Sleep Mix which is also beneficial.

If your busy monkey mind is still keeping you awake, sternly ask or it to "be still" or "be quiet." When I tell my mind, "Be Still," I find it an interesting process to observe. It's like a part of me is listening and actually becomes still.

You can also get a piece of paper and pen and write down all the thoughts you are having on the paper—whatever they are, just let them all come out until your mind has no more words. It might be a lot of writing during the first few times, but this will help release all the thoughts in your mind.

> *Sleep is so important for our wellbeing. Are you willing to make the commitment to yourself, to your body, and begin to turn the light off earlier, to go to bed earlier?*

Chapter 25

God

Any reference to God in this book is referring to what I feel is a vibrant energetic force in the universe, one to be honoured and revered with the deepest of respect. This force is alive and pulsating. What is exciting is we can vibrate however we want with this energy—it is our choice. This energy is pure love; love is everything; and everything is love. It's in the choices that we make which either takes us away from love or brings us towards love, synchronicity, and harmony with the love of God.

There are many religions, beliefs, teachings that are available for us to study and resonate with. I believe they are there to assist us to find our own inner truth. I believe that not one of them is the be-all and end-all, but they are all pathways, roads, or rivers to the greater ocean of divine oneness. As has been said before, all roads lead to the same destination. This is what I truly believe. We are on a journey to experience different things to help us grow and shine. So trust in your path because it's specific to you.

Many of the religions have wonderful teachings if we allow ourselves to be open and explore within them. Sometimes though, throughout humanity and civilisation growing and expanding, people have taken control of those teachings, put their own values and ideas upon them and made them into something different from what was originally intended. Love is love: it has no conditions, no barriers, no limitations. If the teachings don't resonate with you, then move on until you find what does. If, like me, you are inquisitive about this subject, you will find a plethora of different bits of religions that support your beliefs, and that's all you need.

When we look and feel into God on deeper levels, we begin to realise that we are the essence of God; we are love. And when we begin to understand this, we begin to change. Deep reverence is found in our inner being; deep gratitude is found within, and the feeling of awe and inspiration for each moment comes flooding into our awareness.

When we find this deeper meaning to the word God, we begin to understand how we can work with this, how the divine works with us if we so desire it to—and that, my dear readers, is where the magic really begins to happen, for we are purely instruments of the divine, each playing our own tune, and when we are with others, we are all part of a divine orchestra.

Here's a little exercise to help you to connect to your God self. Take the time to do at least three deep breaths. Take your awareness into your heart, and allow your mind to be calm. Breathe in and out a few more times. Ask yourself a question. You may get an answer straight away: trust this answer. You may not get an answer straight away— don't worry. The answer may come at another calm moment or it may come when you are in a meditative state or focusing on something else, like driving or doing the dishes.

God is love
Love is God
You are love
I am love
We are love

Chapter 26

EFT

Emotional Freedom Technique (EFT) is powerful to say the least! I learnt how do it many years ago but didn't fully GET it until my chronic hay fever had left me totally debilitated, and I had to spend the afternoon in bed. I spent an hour or so working with EFT on myself and then—BANG—it was like my body finally got it, and the hay fever dissipated into almost nothing. I can't tell you how overjoyed I still am!

The practice of EFT is widely known and featured in many online resources, but, at that time, I approached it in a different way from the common practices. I approached it from a spiritual perspective, calling upon the teachings and learnings that I have collected on my journey. I felt this was certainly far more powerful than when I had tried it many years prior.

When I finally faced my hay fever in this way, I realised how many layers and levels of energetic blockages that had been in my body, all contributing to the creation of the hay fever I was experiencing.

EFT begins by observing what you are sensing and feeling, so it can be challenging if you are not used to identifying what you feel and sense. However, in saying that, it is an empowering modality that I would always give a go.

EFT works on your meridians, and a gentle tapping on these meridians sends messages to the amygdala in your brain. It begins to identify what you are saying, and it enables you to reprogram the events happening in your body.

When I tap on my body points, I begin by identifying what I am experiencing at present in any level, being physical or emotional.

Once you learn EFT, it gives you the ability to heal yourself for free. You will begin to understand deeper aspects of yourself; it's such an empowering modality. I hope you try it one day.

Chapter 27

Possibilities

You may wonder if this book can help you if you are experiencing stress, anxiety, depression, trauma, cancer, or long-term illnesses. May I assure you that if you are able to do just one of the suggested tools per day, things will begin to change for you (see Chapter 30).

These are the tools that I have taught my clients for the past 10 years and I still continue to do so. After implementing them myself for many years when dealing with my own life situations and trauma, I have found they have offered positive impacts through the many experiences in my life.

I have worked with many people who have had a life of trauma, stress, anxiety, depression, cancer, or long-term illness. By working together, we have made headway. They are now living a more heart-centred life that they would never have believed was possible had they not crossed paths with me and my quirky ways. To me, we were meant to meet and experience what we have experienced. I also believe others meet who they need to meet along the way to assist them. When you are ready, the right teacher comes forth into your life, especially when you have intention. You may have said prayers asking for help and can visualise it happening; that's how it works. It's just wonderful.

Of course, energy healing sessions can support you by cleansing the aura, chakras, and energetic systems. It grounds you and reconnects you to the divine and your own will force. The energy healings give a booster to my clients along the way. This is a good place to start from if you wish to change things in your life. However, by beginning with the suggestions in this book, your life can and will change when you find the willpower to stick with it.

The main thing to remember is that everything is energy: we are energy; we are love. When we look at life and accept we are spiritual beings inside an energetic body, our perspective changes, our reality changes, and we begin to awaken to the possibilities in our life. We realise that we can create heaven on earth here in our own little world.

Never give up.
Have clear intention.
Pray and ask for help and guidance.
Let go and trust you will meet, experience,
or do what is perfectly right for you.

Chapter 28

Daily

In review, the whole essence of this book is to bring to you tools, techniques, and skills to put into place on a daily basis to keep your vibration high so that you are experiencing love, joy, abundance, and whatever else you would like to experience in your life. The real work is finding the inner peace on a day-to-day basis and to operate from that place of peace at all times.

Remember it is totally our choice what we experience. Once we understand this, then we can begin to work with it and bring what we wish to experience into our life. I find this fun, and I hope that you do too.

It is also for when your energy is low, when you are travelling through troubled times, when you are wanting to change your life around, when you are stuck, blocked, and unable to move forward in life. This is for when you have challenges with people around you, you may have trauma or want to move forward in your work, relationships, or any aspect of your life.

If you are able to put these suggestions into action on a daily basis, it will change your life for the better. It's most important to focus on the Rise Above list and to use it when you feel you are heading down the emotional spiral. It's the time that we spend in the lower emotional realm that holds us there: the quicker we can get out using these tools, the quicker you get back into doing what you love: enjoying your life with joy, love, and ease. Your vibration changes and so does everything around you. It's that simple.

Some people ask me, "What do you do each day to assist and allow your day to flow with ease and grace?" All the information within this book is what I do. Whenever I get challenged in my life, I find these tools work. I have shared them with clients and they also find that the techniques work. If things aren't shifting, I use another tool. Each and every technique helps me to move my vibration from one level to another. You need to listen to your body. My routine may not suit you, so it's important to find your own routine. When that routine gets stale, as sometimes it does, then create a new one.

This is my day…

After expressing deep gratitude for everything around me and feeling the essence of gratitude in my body, I take the time to stretch my body, just like a cat or dog does when it gets up. I stretch my spine, my arms, and my legs. I gently twist my arms around and bend over front and back. (A note to the mums and dads out there: Yes, I agree if you've got children crawling all over you first thing in the morning, this is difficult, but have your intention in place each night that this is what you want to do in the morning when you wake up. See what happens, and if you don't have the opportunity that morning, just move forth to the next day. All is well; keep trying or maybe even include the children in the fun.)

Stretching the body allows it to gently awaken and move into place. This stretching really makes me begin to feel alive and it helps me to honour the breath that is going through me. Each morning I feel myself stretching more and more; it feels really good.

I then take some time to do some breathing meditation with presence:

I say Om through each and every chakra, and spend some time focusing on each chakra. I breathe into my chakras and push the stale air out of my lungs. I go through the affirmations of each chakra at the same time.

At this stage, I either do Qigong slapping all over my body, which really wakes me up, or I go for a walk or run the dog around the block.

I also partake in 5 to 10 minutes of sun salutation yoga practices, which I've done for years. On days when I have more time, I like to attend a whole class in the morning.

I call in all of my multi-body systems—ask yourself to bring them in. I connect to Mother Earth and the divine. I ask for guidance and support for my whole day from my guides, the angels, and beings of the light.

I set a clear and strong intention for the day as to what I would like to experience. For example, "It is my intention that my day is filled with joy, peace, and inspiration."

I open my arms and I say with expectation in my heart and whole being, "I wonder what wonderful people I will meet today?" or "I wonder what blessings the universe has in store for me today?" or "I can't wait to experience the joy and laughter in my life today." Anything like that will do.

I put a smile on my face and feel the vibration of the smile, gratitude, and divine bliss through my body. It's going to be a great day today. A simple smile on your mouth is connected to your solar plexus chakra, and it begins to shine. This is your emotional chakra, so smile, smile and smile. If you can't smile, putting a pencil in between your teeth sideways will do the same thing to your solar plexus chakra—go on try it!

If I am challenged at any time throughout the day, I use the techniques in this book to shift me back to a place of inner peace and calm until I'm there.

During the day I will take 5 to 10 minutes to do another meditation, focusing on my breath or perhaps an issue in my life.

At the end of the day, I express gratitude for all I have experienced throughout the day, and I take the time to be curious and look forward to the surprises of the next day that lies ahead.

Of course, it would be challenging to begin with all of these things at once. Changes take time. However, if you want your world to change, then you need to take action. Nothing can happen if you don't take action. If you have a ball, it can't get from A to B unless you either throw it, kick it, push it, or bounce it, but it won't get there if you don't take the action. The actions in this book are simple to do, they are free, and they don't take much time at all. It's about committing to loving yourself, doing something for yourself each day, having the desire to change your life, and doing it.

I pray that you find the life force inside you that supports you to do this. If it's too hard, I suggest you have some Reiki or energy healing to help clear energetic blockages and connect to your will forces.

Take time to sit with the information in this book. Write yourself your own Rise Above list that resonates with you and brings in the things that you feel shift your vibration. I always find that everyone has at least one thing that they love to do that can swiftly change their present emotional and/or physical state.

Once you have written your Rise Above list, gently begin to apply gratitude into your life. Observe yourself, and when you are challenged or your vibration changes, take the time to do one of the things on your list. If that doesn't change anything, choose another and then another. You will find that some will move your emotional and physical state more than others, and they will eventually become your go-to areas for support when you are stuck.

Another practice I do, although not as much as I would like, is called Agnihotra: it is an energetic fire practice which is done in a specially designed copper pyramid. It clears and cleans the entire environment and all that lies within one kilometre of the pyramid's area. I find this practice extremely heart-centred and relaxing. It's really quite magical. You can find information about Agnihotra on the internet.

> **Using your Rise Above list will enable you to change your emotional state at the speed of light, so you can shift yourself into doing what you love with joy and ease instantly.**

Chapter 29

Rise Above List

As mentioned throughout this book, creating a Rise Above list is really important to support you on a daily basis.

The list contains the tools that you can use for yourself when you are stressed, anxious, depressed, overwhelmed, stuck, experiencing trauma, feeling discombobulated, and so on.

Put anything on this list that you feel changes your vibration, in any way or form for the better. Use your Rise Above list when you feel your vibration changing. Refer to it as much as possible until you feel yourself using these tools naturally as an automatic reaction to any situation. Once you have this going, your life will become so much easier, lighter, brighter, and fun.

Sometimes it's fun and more exciting to have a buddy come along with you on the journey. Perhaps you could find someone else to work with so you can support each other. Alternatively, you can join my online groups, in-person groups, or classes where you may find someone who will be your buddy.

I always recommend that the first things to do are the first five on this list, then do what you feel supports you the most or what you intuitively choose.

- Stop
- Breathe
- Hand on heart
- Be present, feel, sense
- Gratitude
- Ask angelic realm for support
- Surrender
- Shining your light exercise
- Ho'oponopono prayer
- Meditation
- Observe your thoughts
- Chant Om
- Get outside into nature
- Move yourself into a different room or place
- Play music that you love
- Dance, run, skip—just move that body
- Sing
- Participate in some gardening
- Hang out with your animals
- Have a cup of tea!
- Qigong slapping
- Phone a friend, a high vibrational one who inspires you

- Read an inspirational book
- Watch an inspirational YouTube video
- Open your mouth, force your tongue out, and say Ahhhh loudly
- Go for a walk
- Do things backwards—it tells the mind that things aren't always the same and to pay attention!
- Have a bath or jump in the river or the sea

You don't have to do all of these, but do the things that support you to shift out of your current emotional state. It may just be one thing, or you may need 10. All is well. You will shift and be better for it.

*Go gentle, one step at a time,
implement one tool at a time.
Get used to it, how does it affect you?
Be present;
enjoy the new vibration supporting you.'*

Chapter 30

 **Gathering it all together**

If you are totally new to just about everything in this book and need some guidance, you can follow the next few pages. If you find you need further support, then please be in touch.

Week 1   Practise stopping and breathing and observing throughout the day.

Week 2   Begin daily gratitude practise in the morning and throughout the day and evening.

Week 3   When challenged in any way, stop, put both hands on your heart, with your arms crossed over your chest; tap your fingers alternatively on your chest.

Week 4   When challenged, stop and be present. Breathe, ask yourself, "What is really happening here?"

Week 5   Begin to incorporate your learnings into everyday life and journal them. What do you notice is changing in your life?

Week 6   Begin to integrate 'shining your light' exercises each morning after your

	gratitude practice and journal what is changing for you.
Week 7	Find a music video of the Ho'oponopono prayer and begin to utilise it for every challenge you have in your life, incorporating what you previously learnt also.
Week 8	Begin to observe your thoughts. What are you saying to yourself? What stories are running in your head? Stop, listen, observe; write them down. Are these thoughts serving you well? If not, it's time to let them go—do not give them any attention. At this stage, you may need to do some inner work on your inner child.
Week 9	Incorporating what you can on a daily basis, begin the practice of Om. Take the time to sit quietly each day and do three Om's. Search on Google for more support.
Week 10	What exercises are you enjoying? Which ones are challenging? Why? What has changed in your life since you began this process?

Each week hereafter, begin to try each of the mentioned suggestions one by one. Some you will enjoy; some may not work for you. Take notice of what shifts in your life. Please try everything so that when you are challenged in life, you have options to choose from. Gather your range and sequence of strategies that best change your vibration.

By the tenth week, you should be getting a fair idea of what works for you and what is just OK. Concentrate on the ones that you know shift you to a higher vibration. If it feels like nothing is changing, then please receive Reiki in person or by distance or engage in some energy work to support you. Feel free to write to me and ask questions if you desire. I'm always happy to help.

Alternatively, one of my readers said she read a chapter per day, then put into practice the teachings of that day. She made a note of what served her well in raising her vibration, and created her own Rise Above list.

Whatever and however this book works for you, just do it. I applaud you immensely for the fact that you are reading it and trying it. It's a hard task changing your ways and by just reading this book, new inspiration is getting into your being. If you want to change, you will put things into practice, whether it be now or in a couple of years. All these methods are tried and tested by myself and my clients. They have created amazing turnarounds from people who had been through stress, anxiety, depression, trauma, bipolar condition, and life-threating illnesses in their lives. All the best, and I'm always here if you need.

Each week, take the time to practise a new technique. Add the new support in the next week and watch your life change around. Enjoy!

PART II

Bring it on...

How to Manifest Your Desires

It's actually simple...

When you know how. The trouble is that a lot of us don't know how. We haven't been shown. The ease and grace of manifesting has not been part of many people's lives. Perhaps our parents and friends have been talking about it, yet our ears haven't opened to what they are actually saying, and our mind hasn't integrated it. It's not until our higher self decides YES! It's time to wake up and listen, and then we actually do. Then life becomes exciting—YES, very exciting!

When you're ready to change life into something new or something different, our first rule of thumb is to stop, observe, witness, and breathe, then we ask ourselves these questions:

What is present for me right now?

Do I want my life to be like this today, tomorrow, and the next day?

Am I ready to make a commitment to myself to change my ways and benefit from my actions?

What choices do I have right now?

Just as described in Part I of this book, we always go back to the breath. We stop; we listen. Then, from there in the stillness, we can make a choice.

The most important action to take, is to put into place, aspects of Part I of this book. It is your guide on how to move your vibration into a place that enables you to manifest what you want in your life. If you are able to put into place the teachings of Part I with everything you do, and allow it to become second nature, then you will naturally begin to connect to your true self and allow your life to flow. The trick is to have these teachings slotted automatically into your subconscious mind, so when things come up for you that you need to move through, you use your Rise Above list and your vibration begins to change.

The second most important part of Part II is your intention; it won't happen without your intention. What you want won't appear if you don't truly desire something to change. Notice the difference between, "I want to change" and "I have the intention to change." This is where the power lies: to have the intention to change is much more powerful, and just this alone can change your life around.

The third most important part is your clarity. If your clarity is not worked on in a simplistic way, then what you want won't appear in your life. Clarity is key to manifesting your desires. When I was manifesting my own home, I was unclear about whether I wanted a swimming pool or an earth-brick house. At the time, I didn't have enough information to assist my vision, and I was unsure about the amount of work both would require. And guess what—I didn't get either because I wasn't clear.

It's actually simple...

The fourth most important part is your faith. I cannot stress how important this is: hold your faith strongly, know that you will receive what you want, then your life will change into what you visualise it to be.

Then once all that is in place, we speak it out to the universe and surrender. Yes, we surrender. We don't talk about it anymore; we don't think about it anymore. We just wait for that magic day when it all begins to happen, and if you have followed the suggestions in this book, then it won't be far away.

Let us begin

For changes to happen in our life, we must take some action. This is proven in science; if one does nothing, nothing can happen. Now the real question is what do we actually do to make things happen?

I spent many years working with mentors, guides, and coaches who helped me with my business and in my life. While these encounters certainly helped me in many aspects, I feel they also held me back because I became very stressed following plans with things I was "meant" to do. The weekly structures, goals, and commitments created significant pressure and an internal guilt where I felt I was not achieving what was expected of me. I wasn't happy doing all these dictated tasks and habits; they slowly created an underlying, uncomfortable vibe within me. I felt stressed and unhappy.

After a few years, I decided to let all this guidance go to allow myself to go with the flow so I could listen to me, so I could be guided by me. I let go and surrendered. I let go of everything. I took a big step back and just allowed myself to be in the flow. I put all of my practices into place, and I learnt how to manifest by myself, using my vibration. As soon as I did this, my life began to change. There was fun and joy and abundance; it was so exciting.

Manifesting what we want in our life is about our vibration. Our vibration is so important. The techniques in Part I teach you how to keep your vibration high—this is key. We cannot attract something different into our lives if our vibration remains the same as it was previously. Each moment of the day, we have to keep our vibration fresh and clear, and we must also be ready and willing to change it as needed.

Remember how some mornings we wake up and we feel heavy, sluggish, not wanting to do anything? Well, we can choose to stay in this space or we can choose to move out of it. We have the power. How do we move out of our current vibration? How can we transcend to another vibration? We go through our Rise Above list, and we keep going through it until our vibration changes and we feel inspired.

Once we begin to feel and experience something different from what we are, this is when we realise that we have the potential to change—but to change into what? And how?

What do you really want? This is a very hard question for a lot of people. It's important to take the time and commit to sitting down and thinking of what you want your life to look like. How about your working week? What would your family time look like? How about your house or where you live? What about your income? It's important to be as specific and honest as possible in this exercise.

Our Vibration

Firstly, observing ourselves in our dark places of despair, fear, worry, anxiety, depression, or worthlessness and wanting to change is key. This creates an intense willpower that will assist you along the way. Sit with these emotions or feelings, feel them in your body, and ask them to show you the way.

They key is to get our energetic vibration into a place where we are able to vibrate with clean, clear energy whilst connected to our heart, so we can put a request out to the universe through our mind. We send this message out there, believing and knowing that it will happen without any doubt whatsoever.

Once we hold this vibration of what we want and how we are going to feel when we get what we want, hold this for a specific amount of time, or longer if needed. If you listen and feel closely, you will feel that you have made a connection with the universe. You will know when you know it, and you'll know that it is yours. It's a feeling; it's a vibration; it's a connection to the divine, like your own attract magnet. This is what you are aiming for with the tools in this book. At first you may not experience

Rise Above Life

this feeling, but once you do, and once you get what you want, you will aim to get this feeling again and again.

Clarity

Clarity is needed from the beginning. Clarity is being really specific and clear about what you want in your life. It is honing what you want down to as few words as possible. I usually begin by writing down words which describe what I want in my life and how it will make me feel.

When we are beginning this process of finding clarity, it is helpful to go through another process first. I suggest this as it assists in the overall vibration in your request for your manifestation.

I call this process the "draft." For the draft, get a big piece of paper and list everything you want—remember to be specific. I try to group similar things together, ie the house or car, wellness, relationship, work life, abundance, etc.

You can draw it if you like or even write a story of what you would like in your house as if it is already in your house in the present moment. Describe how it has everything you need in it. How do you feel in your house? Pretend that you are in the kitchen, what do you see in the kitchen? What do you see when you look out of the window? What's your oven like? What's your benchtop made of? What kind of appliances are there? Be specific—create a story where you are sitting in your desired kitchen. Express what's happening, and most importantly, express how you feel when you have this gorgeous kitchen that you love so much.

I'll write a few examples of some common requests.

Let's say, "My health and wellbeing are not good at present, and I am experiencing pain in my body." In this instance, I would be writing down what I want to feel and how I would like to feel now: "My body is pain free, and I feel fantastic doing the things I love to do."

Avoid going into waffle like, "My headache is gone now" or "I feel my headache getting better." When you're drafting, you are aiming for the end result that you want—nothing more, nothing less! Keep your sentences short, clear, and to the point. You could even just hold, "My body is pain free and I feel fantastic." When you are writing the sentence down, it's important to really feel the words: does the word "fantastic" resonate with you? Or does another word make you feel better, for example, "amazing" or "alive"? It has to be a word that comes from your heart, that makes your feeling body react with some "zing."

Another example: "My bank account balance is forever expanding. This brings me so much joy!" Alternatively, you could name a figure here if you like. It's up to you; it's always up to you: what you desire, what you feel from your heart, and once again, what is the emotion that it brings to you?

How will you feel when you have this amount of money in your bank account?

"I have the most fulfilling relationship, which brings me great joy." Can you feel the simplicity of it all? What is the emotion you want to feel when you have the relationship of your dreams?

When we are working on our clarity, we need to bring all the information into the present—that is, we write it and say it as if we already have it in our lives and are experiencing it now.

This goes for anything you are wanting to manifest in your life. Keep the emotion you want to feel simple, clear, and express it in the present. It can take a little while to get this part right, but once you get the hang of it, you'll be doing OK.

Now, one of the obstacles that holds us back in receiving what we want is our own mind—yes, that's right, our own mind. This resistance usually happens when you begin to question whether you are good enough to receive these things. Perhaps you feel you are not worthy enough to receive these things or when you are trying to work it out, you worry—how will it will come about? I just want you to STOP. That's right—STOP right now. Go to your Rise Above list and change this vibration straight away because this underlying vibration or emotion will cause havoc in your manifesting outcomes. Once you have shifted your vibration, I suggest you start again, and find the clarity.

So, we have stopped and witnessed what is going on in our body; we have listened to our body; we have made an intention to change our life around; we have found the clarity of what we want in our lives, and now we write it all down like this:

It is my intention that I, (your name here), (describe what you want in your life), and this makes me feel...

You don't have to use the exact wording that I have used, but the first line, inserting your name, is the usual format that I use.

Example I: It is my intention that I, Jennie de Vine, my body is healthy, strong, and full of vitality, and this makes me feel so amazing.

Example II: It is my intention that I, Jennie de Vine, I have found my gorgeous life partner, and this makes me feel overjoyed.

Remember, your choice of words is powerful. In these examples, "amazing" and "overjoyed" served as my zing; your words have to make you feel elated.

When we write these, remember that we have already written our list of what we want and the "main words" are a reflection of this, so when I write gorgeous life partner, I have written what I regard as a gorgeous life partner in my draft. If you write you want in your relationship, then these are your words, and they carry the essence of what you want in your life. What each person writes will vary and is up to them as it vibrates what they want in their life.

I trust that is enough examples for you to go by. If not, you can always get in touch with me to work it out.

Once you have this intention, sit quietly with your hand on your heart, making sure you are in a high vibrational state without any negative thoughts or processes going on. If any of these negative energies are present, go back to your Rise Above list and change your state.

It is my intention that I _____
(name here) _____
_____ (have or are experiencing) and it makes me feel _____.

You then clearly state your intention to the universe. Hold the vibration of it for eight minutes. You may feel an energetic shift; you may have thoughts or visions; whatever is just is, as long as it's resonating with you and your intention, all is well.

When you trust and believe that it is yours, let go. Then off you go and do something else.

If you like, you can read this to yourself each day, focusing on your intention, believing, and holding the faith for eight minutes, then relish in the fact that you have it and let it go, and get on with your day.

I did this process for over a year, then one day, after having absolutely nothing, I felt the shift happen. I watched as the energetic cogs of the universe came into play and all of a sudden, I had a house: it was a truly incredible experience.

Extras

Things you can do: Rewrite the story of what you want as often as possible until you reach absolute clarity. It doesn't matter if it changes, but keep the emotional vibration high.

Create a vision board. A vision board is a board of whatever size you like. On it, put images that speak to you about what you want in your life, any images that spark inspiration of the things you want. The key here is to find images that also have a feeling or an emotion attached—you could also add in words. Your images can be drawn by you, found in magazines, or on the internet. Once it's complete, put your vision board somewhere you can look at it daily. Take some time to connect with it, believe you have these things, and then let go, holding the emotion of how you'd like to feel when you have those things in your life.

If you want to rev things up a bit, you could do daily focus on your intention, but it's not essential, especially if you have felt the energetic vibration of you actually having it anyway.

Because that's actually what brings it in.

The process for this is to sit quietly each day for an amount of time. The amount of time depends on you, however studies by Lynne McTaggart have found that there is more power with these sorts of intentions if you multiply your time by eight. So hold your vision and intention for eight minutes, perhaps one time or eight times, it's totally up to you. In Lynn's book, The Power of Eight, she speaks about having eight people holding the intention with you for eight minutes, though I haven't actually tried a manifestation like this. Her writings are not for manifesting "things" as such; she really focuses on world peace, but the way she does it is powerful, and that is what I integrate into my life.

Evolving

Life is so interesting. Just like our DNA, it is forever evolving and expanding. As soon as you learn something that supports you, something else comes into your awareness. I am forever learning. I associate myself with people I love to be around, and whenever we are together, magic happens. I learn so much and my outlook changes. It is very difficult to say, "My book is finished" because life changes in each minute. Each time I reread my book, I want to add some more in. However, this is where it is now. I will leave it here.

Since the writing of this book, I have discovered that one of the most important keys to manifesting what you want in your life is to be doing what you love!

YES! Doing what you love changes your whole vibration around into such an amazing space; you become a magnet for so many wonderful things in your life. So, if you have been unhappy doing what you are doing, and have yearned to do something your whole life, reflect upon that. Perhaps you need to make a shift and do what you love. I promise you,

you'll never regret it. The trust, the hope, the joy: it's all part of the process. Life will reward you.

Wishing you all the very best.

Namaste,
Jennie

Conclusion

"What you have given me is hope." This is the constant message my clients give back to me after they have spent some time with me, usually after my 'Day of Transformation' program. Hope that they can get through, hope that things will change, and are changing, hope that the days ahead are going to be different, and hope and knowing that they can do it. But also they feel supported by me as I offer my presence to be alongside those who work with me in times of need.

If you are able to work your way through this book, putting into place the tips, tools, techniques, and strategies, then you are on your way to a new life, a new way of being and understanding of our mind, emotions, energetic bodies, and how the universe supports you every step of the way.

It's simple, easy to put into place, and best of all— the information is free for all to use.

Acknowledgments

I wish to deeply acknowledge my dear friends and colleagues who have supported me during the writing of this book, especially my dear friend, Sandy Newell, for reminding me that life is for fun; Miranda Wills, who is always an inspiration of pure joy; Julie Grogan, for constantly reminding me that each day is an invitation to be curious; Carla Rose, for honouring of my healing work; Derani, Cath, Melinda, and Jan-Leigh, for the inspiration at my birthday dinner for my book launch. I also wish to thank myself—it's been a huge journey, but I'm here and I've done it!

Deep gratitude to my dear friend Mirakye McCarty for her support, her excitement at my dream coming true, and for offering to have my book launch in her gorgeous shop, Epoche in Kallista.

Gratitude and photo credit to Angela E. Rivas for the photograph of me on the back cover, she always takes a fabulous photo.

Deep thanks to Emily Gowor and Rae Antony, along with the monthly inspirational meet-up group to keep me on track. Yay! My book is alive!

Deepest gratitude to my dearest clients who have trusted in some of my unusual but empowering offerings of guidance from my spiritual perspective on life—for trusting me in my knowledge and wisdom that I share, and sharing the follow-through of their progress after putting the said techniques into action, "I can't wait to read your book." You all have inspired me to keep on keeping on, for it's a challenging task once committed to.

Gratitude to my challenges in life which discombobulated me, and showed me that what I teach works. I had to put into place the teachings many times and "Walk my Talk". Each time it reminded me of something I needed to add—was my book ever going to end?

Deep gratitude to my path in life, to the fire in my belly which spurred this book along in the first place, unable to be ignored. It kept pestering me until I took the action; I'm so glad I did.

Gratitude to my guides, inspirational support, and intuition that has flowed forward. I have been sensing your laughter and guidance along the way, for this book that has come through me, and I've assisted in making it useable to the world at this time.

Gratitude to all my teachers along the way, and the whole of my life! OMG—what a journey, but I'm here, and these tools are how I got through!

Acknowledgments

Gratitude to you, the reader, for taking the time to read my book, and, I hope, putting the tools, tips, and techniques into place. I trust that you are now experiencing life from a different perspective and are having so much fun and joy in your life. I so look forward to hearing from you and your experiences of putting my Rise Above list into action.

Many blessings to all, much Love and Light 💜⭐💜
Jennie

About the Author

Jennie de Vine is a passionate mother of four lovely children and three star babies, intent on finding her truth, shining her light, and sharing with others so they too can shine.

As soon as Jennie was introduced to spirituality, she was like a dry sponge soaking up every bit of information. This path led her into the studies of natural therapies, focusing on energy healing, spiritual healing, Reiki, and many other alternative supportive therapies along the way.

Jennie believes that everything is energy; we are spiritual beings, first and foremost, housed inside a physical body. Her work comes from her understanding of the spiritual self and how healing in this realm greatly affects your physical, emotional, mental, and spiritual self, enabling you to live a fuller, more present, and purposeful life.

Jennie experienced chronic fatigue for 10 years, during which she was unable to move for four months. Throughout this time, she learnt a lot about the power of our mind and how to work with your thoughts to change your life around. She did this then and continues to do so now when challenges come her way.

With tenacity and faith, she held a dream for 33 years close to her heart. When the opportunity rose, she manifested her dream into reality by founding the Diamond Light Healing Centre located in Warburton. She wanted to establish a haven where people can come and stay, receive healing, or do her transformational workshops. Energy healing and gardening are her passions and learning tools. Life's experiences and her intention on focusing on her truth gave her the lessons she needed to share with others.

Jennie de Vine
Diamond Light Healing Centre
2b Louis Ave, Warburton Melbourne

https://www.diamondlighthealingcentre.com.au

What Jennie offers

Day of Transformation retreat

* Five hours of self-love totally dedicated to yourself. We work through your current issues. We connect to find solutions, to move forward in your life, and to clear blockages in many aspects of your life.
* A delicious organic vegan meal together.
* A refreshing stroll along the beautiful O'Shannassy Aqueduct Trail in the gorgeous Yarra Valley.
* Nurturing energy healing session for deep relaxation.

It's the best program if you'd like to press the 'reset' button for your life, redefine your life, regain your centre, your energy, and your divine purpose.

This day is also suited to carers.

Energy Healing sessions

A combination of spiritual healing, Reiki, Sekhem (ancient Egyptian Healing) process work, inner child work, working in the past, present, and future with different modalities, including NLP (Neuro-Linguistic

Programming), counselling, intuitive guidance, hope, and much more.

Distant Energy Healing sessions

These sessions are also available online from the comfort of your home. Many clients book these when they are unable to get to Warburton.

Cancer Support Program

If you are going through cancer, Jennie offers positive support from an energetic perspective.

Information and testimonials can be found www.diamondlighthealingcentre.com.au

Are you with NDIS?

Many of these clients have never felt the calm and serenity in their mind as they do after a working with Jennie.

Accomodation

Accomodation is also available at Jennie's 'Diamond Light Retreat' in the gorgeous Yarra Valley, bookings through Airbnb or direct with Jennie.

www.ingramcontent.com/pod-product-compliance
Lightning Source LLC
Chambersburg PA
CBHW051537010526
44107CB00064B/2755